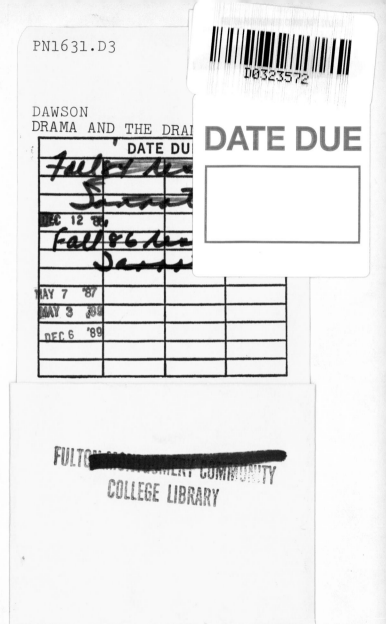

The Critical Idiom

Founder Editor: JOHN D. JUMP (1969–1976)

---

11 Drama and the Dramatic

Drama & the Dramatic/*S. W. Dawson*

Methuen & Co Ltd

First published 1970
by Methuen & Co Ltd
11 New Fetter Lane, London EC4P 4EE
Reprinted twice
Reprinted 1979

© 1970 S. W. Dawson

Reproduced Photolitho in Great Britain
by J. W. Arrowsmith Ltd, Bristol

ISBN 0 416 17280 6

For my Father

Contents

General Editor's Preface

The volumes composing the Critical Idiom deal with a wide variety of key terms in our critical vocabulary. The purpose of the series differs from that served by the standard glossaries of literary terms. Many terms are adequately defined for the needs of students by the brief entries in these glossaries, and such terms do not call for attention in the present series. But there are other terms which cannot be made familiar by means of compact definitions. Students need to grow accustomed to them through simple and straightforward but reasonably full discussions. The main purpose of this series is to provide such discussions.

Many critics have borrowed methods and criteria from currently influential bodies of knowledge or belief that have developed without particular reference to literature. In our own century, some of them have drawn on art-history, psychology, or sociology. Others, strong in a comprehensive faith, have looked at literature and literary criticism from a Marxist or a Christian or some other sharply defined point of view. The result has been the importation into literary criticism of terms from the vocabularies of these sciences and creeds. Discussions of such bodies of knowledge and belief in their bearing upon literature and literary criticism form a natural extension of the initial aim of the Critical Idiom.

Because of their diversity of subject-matter, the studies in the series vary considerably in structure. But all authors have tried to give as full illustrative quotation as possible, to make reference whenever appropriate to more than one literature, and to write in such a way as to guide readers towards the short bibliographies in which they have made suggestions for further reading.

John D. Jump

University of Manchester

Preface

The critical idiom – is there only one? The question needs to be faced. Johnson was a great critic, from whom we can learn a great deal, but feeling our way into his idiom is a labour of literary and historical imagination, from which we emerge with a sharpened consciousness that *we* couldn't express ourselves in it. Even Arnold, so much nearer to us in time, forces us to realize that however valuable we consider the emphasis implied in 'poetry is a criticism of life' it is hardly a phrase we would use without the inverted commas. What we have taken from Johnson or Arnold we have translated into our own idiom, the idiom of modern English criticism.

That idiom is the words and phrases we use in talking about literature; it is the condition of our understanding one another, and derives from the tradition of modern criticism. That 'we', of course, raises difficulties, for the decision *what is* the central tradition of modern criticism is in itself a critical judgement which cannot be dodged. The idiom (this we can see more clearly as a result of our reading of Johnson and Arnold) is never a mere set of descriptive terms, since it implies standards, values and preferences. A critical term which continues to be used over the centuries, like 'conceit', changes its meaning with the dominant literary preferences of the age, which are never, of course, 'purely' literary preferences. Other words, and 'drama' and 'dramatic' are among these, change from being almost neutrally descriptive terms (drama = plays, dramatic = characteristic of plays) and take on, within the prevalent tradition, strong implications of approbation or disapprobation. What strikes one particularly in reading modern criticism is the frequency with which the adjective 'dramatic' is used with reference to literature other than plays – dramatic irony in Chaucer, 'the novel as a dramatic poem', dramatic language in Donne's poetry and so on. We find in modern critical usage such a pervasive use of the term and others closely related to it that if Johnson were able to return and scrutinize modern criticism he would find it initially quite as puzzling as we find his own characterization of the pastoral mode of *Lycidas* – 'easy, vulgar, and therefore disgusting'.

Writing about the modern critical tradition in an 'objective' fashion presents the same problems as face the anthropologist who attempts to analyse the culture of which he is a part and whose language he shares. Particularly one becomes aware of the interdependence of concepts, what Wittgenstein somewhere calls a 'nest of propositions'. 'Dramatic' in modern criticism is vitally connected with a whole body of other terms – 'situation', 'response', 'tension', 'concrete' and 'presentment' for example – and with an unprecedented (historically speaking) stress on irony and the central importance of metaphor. Wimsatt and Brooks, in their *Literary Criticism: a Short History*, go so far as to find in all this what they call a dramatic or 'dramatistic' theory of poetry (see particularly pp. 673–5).

To trace the development of this cluster of concepts, to make as clear as possible the assumptions about literature and the way it is creative which are implied, would involve a full-scale history of modern criticism, an examination of what such critics as T. S. Eliot, G. Wilson Knight and F. R. Leavis have in common and how they differ. Such a study would be valuable, but it would not belong to the present series. What I have proposed to myself is something much simpler. Making the natural assumption that the literary qualities which 'drama', 'dramatic' and related terms are used to point to are in some essential way inherent in drama as it has been traditionally understood, I have begun there, and tried to show what is inherent in our response to drama. I have then attempted a brief discussion of the light this throws on contemporary critical usage, instancing in particular the critical work of F. R. Leavis.

Shakespeare is central to this short study, because he is our greatest dramatist, because his plays are most generally available, but primarily because I believe that it is only with reference to Shakespeare that the tradition of modern criticism can be understood. It is worth considering why this is not true of the criticism of Johnson or Arnold.

I have attempted to acknowledge indebtedness to published works in the body of the text and in the bibliography. To my students, colleagues and friends, and those with whom I have worked for many years in the amateur theatre I am greatly indebted; particularly to David Sims, Ian Robinson and Anne Samson for their conversation and writing. My gratitude for the late Professor J. D. Jump's understanding and good will must be shared by all who knew him. My wife has helped in so many ways that an autobiography would be the sole adequate acknowledgement.

I
Drama, Theatre and Reality

I

Else a great prince in prison lies

Everybody, one is tempted to say, knows what a play is. Experience of children at home and at school shows how early the idea of 'a play' develops from the apparently instinctive 'playing at' adult activities and concerns. Imaginative teaching of the very young has demonstrated the educational value of writing and acting plays, and of various kinds of impromptu drama. On the other hand the experience of teachers also shows that the proportion of children who eventually progress to *reading* plays with enjoyment and understanding, as they would read novels, is remarkably small. It appears that an appreciation of plays in performance is almost universal, but that reading plays is a sophisticated activity. The very ability to read a play with understanding depends, moreover, on prior knowledge of what a performance of a play is like. Everything seems to point to the primacy of performance.

What, then, are we to make of *this*, coming as it does from one of the greatest critics in the language? 'A dramatic exhibition is a book recited with concomitants that increase or diminish its effect' (Johnson, *Preface to Shakespeare*). Johnson's definition was not, of course, intended to be exhaustive; it has its place in a particular argument, and carries the emphasis he desires for his particular purpose. However, words like 'exhibition', 'recited' and 'concomitants' are hardly likely to recall to us the experience of one of Shakespeare's plays in a satisfactory performance. The simple 'a book', indeed, raises a number of questions, more particularly, what sort of 'book'? Certainly not *any* sort. On the contrary, a particular kind of book, a play. If the book is not dramatic, the 'exhibition' will not be dramatic either. To determine what is drama, what is dramatic, is to be concerned with books; that is, the criteria are ultimately literary.

To become thus entangled in apparent contradictions is a necessary condition of embarking on any discussion of drama. In a study of this nature I shall, of course, be primarily concerned with dramatic literature *as* literature, but what I have to say is dependent throughout on an understanding of what a play in performance is, and how the nature of plays has been, and will continue to be, determined by the conditions under which they might be acted. We cannot escape from the paradoxical truth that a play unacted remains somehow incomplete, despite the fact that any one performance of the play may be so untrue to its spirit and meaning as to be positively unhelpful to our understanding of it. Any dispute as to the meaning and interpretation of a play takes us back to the words. 'The lines of the play are the only guides a good director or actor needs' (Suzanne K. Langer, *Feeling and Form*, p. 315). In our reading of plays we are placing ourselves, for the most part unconsciously, in the position of the producer and his entire company of actors, and any critical discussion of a play that is not in some sense the sketch of a production is not likely to enhance our understanding. This does not imply that any reasonably intelligent reader could produce or act in the play in question; but on the other hand neither a talent for acting nor a command of all the skills of a theatrical producer is in itself a qualification for pronouncing on drama, as the published utterances of actors and producers daily testify. What can be said is that the producer and actor are often forced to answer questions which either do not occur to readers, or which readers are content to leave unanswered. A reader may, for instance, persuade himself that he has understood a particular speech, though the necessity for actually delivering it would quickly undeceive him; to be placed in the position where stress, tone and gesture must be imaginatively determined, if it does not sharpen one's understanding, at least puts an edge on the consciousness of one's impercipience. Indeed one can go further, for in acting a dramatic speech the reader is liberated from those physical restraints and emotional inhibitions which often limit his response to a work of literature to the merely cerebral. Dramatic literature requires a responsiveness, not just of mind, but of the whole body, so that only in performance (solitary though that performance may be) does the whole work realize itself. This is a matter which will require closer investigation and at this point one example must suffice. Consider Macbeth's great soliloquy in Act V, Scene v.

> Tomorrow, and tomorrow, and tomorrow,
> Creeps in this petty pace from day to day,
> To the last syllable of recorded time;
> And all our yesterdays have lighted fools
> The way to dusty death. Out, out, brief candle!
> Life's but a walking shadow, a poor player
> That struts and frets his hour upon the stage
> And then is heard no more. It is a tale
> Told by an idiot, full of sound and fury
> Signifying nothing.

How is one to read it so as fully to realize what is implicit in it? It expresses that extreme of apathy which is despair; the word 'tomorrow' is robbed of its customary flavour of anticipation or potentiality, so that the sense we get of pointless repetition causes a progressive lowering of pitch throughout the first line. This lowering of pitch brings (if we give our bodies over to the verse) a corresponding lowering of the arm, so that at the end of the line the arm hangs limp, the hand pointing to the ground on which the 'petty pace' creeps. Similarly the sweeping, surveying gesture of 'all our yesterdays' leads again to the limp pointing to the ground of 'dusty death'. Analysed in this way the whole speech implies a number of desperate gestures towards light or fullness (the first 'tomorrow', 'all', 'lighted', 'candle', 'tale') all of which decline into the limp downward gesture, with bowed head, of 'creeps', 'dusty', 'shadow', 'stage' (which is actually down there to be pointed to) and 'nothing'. These are only brief and crude indications, but they help one to understand the difference, in the theatre, between the actor using the words to achieve some effect, and the actor allowing the words to speak through him. (Although that way of putting it could be misleading, as indicating passivity; the actor is, in fact, a very active collaborator with the language.)

Anyone who has had the experience of acting in an indifferently translated play will know the feeling that the language is letting one down – that the full life and body of it has somehow escaped in the process of translation. What conceivable translation, for instance, could render the full dramatic life, instinct with expression, movement and gesture, of a passage like this?

> Que ces vains ornements, que ces voiles me pèsent!
> Quelle importune main, en formant tous ces nœuds,
> A pris soin sur mon front d'assembler mes cheveux?
> Tout m'afflige et me nuit, et conspire à me nuire.
>
> (Racine, *Phèdre* I, iii)

Racine is notoriously difficult to translate; one of the best modern English versions gives us:

> How these vain jewels, these veils weigh on me!
> What meddling hand has sought to rearrange

My hair, by braiding it across my brow?
All things contrive to grieve and thwart me, all.
(John Cairncross's translation, in *Phaedra and other plays*, Penguin ed.,
Harmondsworth, 1963.)

Apart from the fact that the rhythmical impetus is slowed, and in the first line to disastrous effect, the passion of this is reduced to mere irritability. The sense of Phèdre's being surrounded by entirely inimical and oppressive circumstances, which is what a dramatic performance would grow out of (Phèdre turning, indeed writhing, from this side to that in order to find a way out of her situation) is conveyed by words like 'nœuds', which carries suggestions absent from 'braiding', by the military suggestions of 'front' and 'assembler' (she is besieged, beset on all sides) and by the insistent 'i' sounds in the final line, which reinforce this suggestion. The original passage requires an actress to yield herself to its movement and implications; the translation, though 'faithful' enough, offers little assistance, and at times is a positive hindrance.

Not everyone who is interested in dramatic literature is temperamentally inclined to take a practical part in dramatic activities, nor is everyone in a position to witness performances of the dramatic classics as often as he night wish. However, the advantage is not always with the practical 'man of the theatre', who is very much open to the temptation to aim at particular theatrical effects, which are imposed on the play rather than growing out of it. As soon as considerations of effect, and a consciousness of the audience as a body of spectators whose feelings can be played upon, become predominant the play is regarded as a means rather than an end. Theatrical as opposed to dramatic thinking is essentially mechanistic. Consider, for instance, the following passage from Dryden's discussion of his own *All for Love*.

The greatest error in the contrivance seems to be in the person of Octavia; for, though I might use the privilege of a poet, to introduce

B

her into Alexandria, yet I had not enough considered, that the compassion she moved to herself and children was destructive to that which I reserved for Antony and Cleopatra; whose mutual love being founded upon vice, must lessen the favour of the audience to them, when virtue and innocence were oppressed by it. And, though I justified Antony in some measure, by making Octavia's departure to proceed wholly from herself; yet the force of the first machine still remained; and the dividing of pity, like the cutting of a river into many channels, abated the strength of the natural stream.

Dryden might be discussing a hydro-electric power-station. Indeed, his dramatic essays, though very derivative and only intermittently disinterested, mark a crucial deterioration in the history of English drama. The whole theory of the Restoration heroic play is a curious blend of the literary and the theatrical, with a revealing stress on 'admiration' as the end of serious drama. It belongs to an age when theatrical effects for their own sake had virtually usurped the stage, and inaugurates the period of over a hundred years in which Shakespeare's tragedies were presented in what seem to us ludicrously mutilated versions. It is in such a context that we must understand Dr Johnson's remarkable strictures on Shakespearian tragedy, and his willingness to discuss Addison's fossil-play *Cato* in the same breath. (Though Johnson, with his famous appeal from art to nature, is capable of seeing how undramatic *Cato* is; in his *Life* of Addison: '. . . it is rather a poem in dialogue than a drama, rather a succession of just sentiments in elegant language than a representation of natural affections, or of any state probable or possible in human life.')

It would be wearisome to examine the succession of plays, and the burden of so-called 'daring and imaginative' production effects, which a dominant concern with 'theatre' is responsible for. Clearly the mere performer, as well as the mere reader, is liable to certain limitations in discussing drama. But the ideal commentator on drama would combine a scrupulous critical concern with the text

with as close a concern as possible with the necessities and potentialities of actual performance.

II

... to hold, as 'twere, the mirror up to nature

One of the most recurrent and least profitable arguments about
drama has centred on the nature of dramatic 'illusion'. Aristotle's
placing of drama among the imitative arts gave rise during the
Renaissance to the idea that an audience was in some sense deluded
or deceived into believing that what happened on the stage was
'really' happening, and that drama should be limited as far as
practicable by the possibilities and probabilities of 'real life'. This
led to the promulgation of the unities of time and place, which, in
their extreme form, would have limited the duration of the action
to the duration of the performance, and the place to a single area
equal to the area of the stage. This is not the place to explore the
confusions and contradictions to which the idea gave rise, many of
which are apparent in Dryden's essays; the whole absurd structure
is demolished in a few pages of Johnson's *Preface to Shakespeare*.
'It is false, that any representation is mistaken for reality; that any
dramatic fable in its materiality was ever credible, or, for a single
moment, was ever credited. . . . It will be asked how the drama
moves, if it is not credited. It is credited with all the credit due to a
drama.' Johnson bases his defence of Shakespeare from the confused theorists on the same principle as Sidney's defence of poetry
from the confused moralists: 'Now, for the poet, he nothing
affirms, and therefore never lieth.'

The unities did not, in England, survive Johnson's assault,
backed as it was by the authority of Shakespeare. But the technical
development of the theatre made possible an increasing degree of
naturalism in stage settings, so that by the early twentieth century

it came to be accepted that, for a modern play at least, the norm was a picture-frame stage so arranged as to resemble as closely as possible a room with one wall removed, on which the actors reproduced the actions and speech of 'real life'. The drama which belonged most naturally in this theatre dealt with social problems in a predominantly middle-class milieu; the name of Ibsen was invoked in its cause.

The decline of this kind of drama (which until very recently dominated the commercial theatre at least) is the central thread that runs through the history of modern drama, and it would be impossible here to enumerate all the various forces which contributed to it. Poets like Yeats objected to the banishing from the theatre of poetic speech; others pointed to the possibilities of non-naturalistic movement, as in the ballet, and some producers desired more 'aesthetic' visual effects. Social revolutionaries criticized the implicitly bourgeois nature of the form, and from another point of view the affinities between drama and ritual were much canvassed. But in England, and to a great extent on the continent too, the most important single influence was Shakespeare. Research into the nature of Shakespeare's theatre, by scholars who were also concerned with the practice of drama, convinced them that the late nineteenth-century manner of producing Shakespeare in naturalistic settings distracted attention from the language, and broke up the dramatic continuity. It is from these researches, and the practical experiments that followed, that our understanding of the nature of dramatic convention derives.

The basis of such an understanding is the recognition that the action is the language, that the language creates the dramatic 'world' of the play, and that the relation between this world and reality is metaphorical. The nature of the stage, therefore, the settings and the style of acting, should be such as to assist the language in its creation of this metaphorical world. The *language* of a play establishes for the audience what are the criteria of possi-

bility and probability; movement, gesture, properties and scenery
are auxiliaries which, ideally speaking, should *grow out of* the
creative language.

The principle may perhaps be best illustrated by the plays of
Ibsen. No one today would consider Ibsen as primarily a social-
problem dramatist; his drama has outlived the social circumstances
in which it was produced. But dramatically Ibsen belongs to a
particular world, the dominant *poetic* reality of which is houses and
rooms. One thinks of *The Doll's House*, of *Rosmersholm* (the name
of a house), of the attic in *The Wild Duck*, and of John Gabriel
Borkman's footsteps penetrating oppressively into the room
below. Many of Ibsen's characters muffle themselves compulsively
in a room or a house against the danger and freedom of life outside.
The whole complex way in which, in that great play *The Master
Builder*, houses and towers become the primary antagonistic sym-
bols, is a culmination of Ibsen's dramatic vision. A whole room,
with the suggestion of a whole house leading off from it, is thus an
essential frame for the world which Ibsen's language creates, and
is as it were the basic unit of his dramatic imagination. It is interesting to follow the dramatist, in his later plays, gradually moving
away from rooms and houses into the open air, at the same time
stretching the resources of the naturalistic theatre until, in *When
We Dead Wake*, we come across this stage-direction;

> Suddenly there is a roar like thunder from high in the snows. The
> avalanche slides down at a terrific pace. Professor Rubek and Irena
> are dimly seen as they hurtle down in the mass of snow and are buried
> under it.

Nothing could illustrate better (though there are instances in
Shakespeare) the love-hate relationship between the great dramatist
and the exigencies of the practical theatre than the preposterous
demands implied in this single stage-direction.

We find it useful to talk of the conventions of a particular type of theatre in a particular age, and a prior knowledge of these conventions can prevent a deal of misunderstanding. Yet even within the same general form, as for instance Jacobean tragedy, the precise conventions to obtain are created by the language of the particular play. We are not likely today to be disconcerted or annoyed by the use of the 'aside', but in accepting it as a dramatic convention we must be careful to distinguish between different ways in which it can be used. In Tourneur's *The Revenger's Tragedy* it is often a direct nudge to the audience, an invitation to share a character's delight in a particularly ingenious or ironic stroke, to remind us that a character is only playing a part, or to make a direct moral comment on the action. In Middleton's *The Changeling* and *Women Beware Women*, on the other hand, the aside is much nearer the interior monologue of the novelist, a glimpse into the complexities of motive and self-deceit which underly the surface action. Tourneur and Middleton both belong to their age, but the significance of Tourneur's dramatic world, like that of Jonson's, is on the surface; Middleton (it is this which has struck some critics as remarkably modern) explores the hinterland of unconscious or only half-recognized desires. The essential difference in the way the convention is used can be understood only through an examination of the language.

III

Rejection of the idea of delusion, and an understanding of the nature of convention does not, however, entirely settle the problems which have become attached to the nature of what is often called 'dramatic illusion'. Coleridge, for instance, made a number of attempts to clarify his dissatisfaction with Johnson's commonsense position, and to give a satisfactory account of what he called 'stage-illusion'. Thus: 'The true stage-illusion . . . consists – not in the mind's judging it to be a forest, but, in its remission of the judgement that it is not a forest.' And again: 'In evincing the impossibility of delusion, [Johnson] makes no sufficient allowance for an intermediate state, which I have before distinguished by the term, illusion, and have attempted to illustrate its quality and character by reference to our mental state when dreaming. In both cases we do not simply judge the imagery to be unreal; there is a negative reality, and no more. Whatever, therefore, tends to prevent the mind from placing itself, or being placed, gradually in that state in which the images have such negative reality for the auditor, destroys the illusion, and is dramatically improbable.' I am not sure how helpful all this really is; does it in fact take us further than Johnson's 'It is credited with all the credit due to a drama'? The comparison with dream-states, at any rate, would lead us further into the realms of psychology than would be desirable here. There are, however, certain resemblances between this approach and that of a modern philosopher of art, Suzanne K. Langer, who gives to the term 'illusion' a specific meaning other than what we might call its vulgar one.

As for the motif of illusion, it is generally coupled with its opposite, reality, and serves rather to raise difficulties than to solve them. . . . The problem of illusion is treated from the critic's point of view as a demand on our credulity, our willingness to 'make-believe'. . . . The function of artistic illusion is not 'make-believe', as many philosophers and psychologists believe, but the very opposite, disengagement from belief – the contemplation of sensory qualities without their usual meanings of 'Here's that chair', 'That's my telephone', 'These figures ought to add up to the bank's statement', etc. The knowledge that what is before us has no practical significance in the world is what enables us to give attention to its appearance as such.

(Op. cit., pp. 13, 15, 49)

This particular passage refers particularly to the visual arts, but its bearing on drama is clear. Without proceeding further into the realm of aesthetics I shall take up the hint of Miss Langer's 'attention'.

It is characteristic of drama, as of no other form of literature, that it makes an absolute and sustained demand on our attention. A poem or a novel can be, indeed often must be, put down and taken up again as we are interrupted or distracted; we can re-read parts of it, or turn back to remind ourselves of some earlier passage. A play in performance demands our uninterrupted attention, not only for our own sakes, but for the sake of other members of the audience. Sitting in silence without conspicuous movement for as long as an hour and a half is a considerable achievement, possible for most of us only when our attention is entirely engrossed. It follows that the dramatist's primary responsibility is to seize and hold our attention. This is why we commonly refer to plays and films as 'gripping'.

It will be useful at this point to examine the way in which the words 'drama' and 'dramatic' are used in common speech outside the context of literature or the theatre. We may speak, for instance, of 'a dramatic moment'. Imagine yourself one of a roomful of people, at a party for instance, standing and talking in groups. Suddenly the door opens and a woman stands in the doorway. She looks round the room, and her gaze settles on a man standing at the far end of the room. He looks at her as she closes the door behind her and moves slowly across the room. This is in itself a thoroughly commonplace happening, and might well attract no attention whatsoever; it is not, in itself, dramatic. Yet let us imagine further that the man and woman are known to you, and that the man has already told you of a quarrel they have had on the way to the party, after which she has insisted on his continuing alone. Add to this your knowledge of the grounds of the quarrel, her jealousy of another woman who is also in the room. Given that her entrance has attracted your attention, her survey of the room and her approach to the man, arousing in you certain expectations or forebodings, will give rise in you to a certain tension; it will be, for you, a dramatic moment; you will be an audience of one to a scene in which everyone else is an actor, and this basic scene is capable of taking on an increasing complexity and depth. You may, 'for instance, know something about the attitude of the second woman which neither of the two main actors is aware of. And so on. . . .

Here is another example – the newspaper headline 'Minister's dramatic intervention in wage dispute'. The implications of this are (1) the intervention was unexpected; thus our attention is seized. (2) It has created a new and interesting situation. (3) The situation takes its meaning and interest from a certain context; it is part of an 'action' that has a beginning (which we know) and must lead to some end (which we do not know). The journalist's aim is to seize and hold our attention, beginning with a single unexpected and startling act, and going on to make us aware of certain possibilities inherent in the situation created by that act. But, if he is a good journalist, he knows that our interest will not be long held by one set of possibilities – tomorrow's story must give us another situation, with a slightly different set of possibilities, lest we quickly become bored by it all. To keep his readers' expectations aroused over a number of days, and to bring the story to a satisfactory conclusion, the journalist makes it into an 'action'; a satisfactory conclusion here is one which will not cause us to be disappointed when, on opening our newspaper next day, we do not find the story continued. A newspaper story has more in common with drama than has an ordinary story, since the writer is concerned with immediacy, a sense of its happening *now*, not in the past. (Headlines are usually in the present tense.) This immediacy is integral to drama, since what is happening on the stage is happening now, for the first time, and not in what Suzanne Langer calls the 'virtual past' of narrative literature.

The duration of the action is limited to the time during which our attention can be held, and there are limits to the duration of a play which do not apply to a poem or a novel. Aristotle in the *Poetics* observes that 'a certain length is necessary, and a length that can easily be embraced by the memory', and the Italian Renaissance critic Castelvetro related the length of a play to the 'physical necessities' of audience and actors. Indeed the necessary limitations of memory, hunger and fatigue, to particularize no further, could, not only in oneself but in other members of the audience, contribute to the failure of that concentrated attention which drama requires of us.

A dramatic action then, to return to Aristotle, must be 'of a certain length' and have 'a beginning, a middle and an end'. It embraces a series of situations which compel our attention; each situation arises out of what has preceded it, and gives rise to expectation of further change until the end of the action, which is in Johnson's words 'the end of expectation'. Some such simple formulation is as far as one can go without considering the medium in which situation and action are created – dramatic language.

2

Language and Situation

I

'... there is, of course, about Donne's characteristic poetry – in the presentment of situations, the liveliness of enactment – something fairly to be called dramatic.' In his characterization of Donne's verse in *Revaluation* Dr Leavis points in particular to the way in which 'utterance, movement and intonation are those of the talking voice'. Colloquial language is easier to recognize than describe, but we can also point to what kinds of language are *not* dramatic.

> Of Man's first disobedience, and the fruit
> Of that forbidden tree whose mortal taste
> Brought death into the World, and all our woe,
> With loss of Eden, till one greater Man
> Restore us, and regain the blissful seat,
> Sing, Heavenly Muse. . . .
>
> *(Paradise Lost* Bk I, ll. 1–6)

This is deliberate and measured, a fusion of oration and prayer, and its structure, in which the main verb does not appear until the sixth line, depends on a subordination of parts that is foreign to the spoken language, in which sentence-structure is much looser. But Milton is something of an extreme case. Perhaps Dryden provides us with a less obvious example, since we have Hopkins' testimony that in his verse is to be found the 'naked thew and sinew' of the language.

> In pious times, ere priest-craft did begin,
> Before polygamy was made a sin;

> When Man on many multiplied his kind,
> Ere one to one was cursedly confined,
> When Nature prompted, and no law denied
> Promiscuous use of concubine and bride;
> Then Israel's monarch, after Heaven's own heart,
> His vigorous warmth did, variously, impart
> To wives and slaves: and, wide as his command,
> Scattered his maker's image through the land.
>
> (*Absalom and Achitophel*, ll. 1–10)

This is more relaxed and less deliberate, but not therefore more dramatic. It is an accomplished narrative style, and we are conscious of the narrator's tact and strategy in handling what is, after all, a rather tricky subject. Charles II's promiscuity is part of the comedy, but he must not be allowed to appear in a ridiculous light. The rapid narrative flow carries us on to the crucial verb 'scattered' (with its implications of god-like generosity) and all the preceding verbs are muted by their subordination to this progress. We register an admirably calculated effect. The opening lines of Pope's *Epistle to Arbuthnot*, on the other hand, are strikingly dramatic.

> Shut, shut the door, good John! fatigued, I said,
> Tie up the knocker, say I'm sick, I'm dead.
> The Dog-star rages! nay 'tis past a doubt,
> All Bedlam, or Parnassus, is let out:
> Fire in each eye, and papers in each hand,
> They rave, recite, and madden round the land.
> What walls can guard me, or what shades can hide?
> They pierce my thickets, through my Grot they glide;
> By land, by water, they renew the charge;
> They stop the chariot, and they board the barge.
> No place is sacred, not the Church is free;
> Even Sunday shines no Sabbath-day to me;
> Then from the Mint walks forth the man of rhyme,
> Happy to catch me just at dinner-time.

This consists, in fact, of a series of exclamations forced from the poet by intrusions on his privacy. He evokes a situation of siege, and his reaction to it is one of comic exasperation – the exaggeration of it (especially in the metaphorical warfare of lines 6 to 10) implying the comment, 'Yes, you may well laugh, but this is the way I am driven to express myself.' The outburst seems to invite the response, 'Come, it can't be as bad as all that!' to be followed by, 'Oh can't it? just listen to this then!' The passage enacts restless, desperate and exasperated movement, gesture and expression, to be concluded, perhaps, by the speaker's exhausted collapse into a chair with a helpless throwing apart of the arms. It does not, in short, describe a situation, it presents or enacts it; to put it another way, the language *is* the situation because it strikes us as having been compelled from the speaker.

It is this last characteristic which is so apparent in the poetry of Donne.

> I wonder by my troth, what thou, and I
> Did, till we loved? were we not weaned till then?
> But sucked on country pleasures, childishly?
> Or snorted we in the seven sleepers' den?
> 'Twas so; but this, all pleasures fancies be.
> If ever any beauty I did see,
> Which I desired, and got, 'twas but a dream of thee.
>
> *(The Good-morrow)*

This is both exclamatory and interrogative, that is, it demands attention and requires response. It gives an impression, not only of someone speaking, but of someone being spoken to, and like the Pope passage it seems to have been compelled from the speaker by his situation. It is worth noting how much of the language of drama is exclamatory, interrogative or imperative.

There are other points of resemblance between the two passages which are worth pointing to. One notices in particular the importance of active verbs, the violence of Pope's 'rave, recite and madden', the dismissive force of Donne's 'sucked' and 'snorted'.

Consider how, in the Donne, the strong verbs 'see' and 'got', although in a strict sense grammatically subordinate, are dramatically liberated by their stress, and the relative weakness of ' 'twas'.

The way in which language creates situation and embodies action can be seen in another of Donne's poems, *The Sun Rising*. The initial exasperation of 'Busy old fool, unruly sun', is typical, but we may soon be driven to ask ourselves why he is talking to the sun at such length. The answer, of course, is that he is talking *at* the sun but *to* his mistress, of whose presence we are kept continually aware. They have been wakened by the sun, he has turned towards the window, and, keenly aware of his appreciative audience of one, launches into a virtuoso denunciation intended to entertain her (Donne is 'showing off' as usual) to flatter her ('But that I would not lose her sight so long') and to persuade her that the sun's having risen is no reason for them to leave their bed, which has during the course of the poem usurped from the sun the prestige of being the centre of the universe. The action of the poem moves gradually from the sun to the bed, so that by the end of it the poet has turned his back on the sun, and is devoting his entire attention to his mistress. Everything the sun represents has been either absorbed or dismissed; the whole world of varied human activity outside the bedroom (vividly evoked in a few lines) is reduced to insignificance as Donne makes 'one little room an everywhere'. The whole poem has an action with a beginning, a middle and an end, the 'right true end' of love.

George Herbert's *The Collar* is probably one of the finest examples in English of the way in which dramatic language can create an action within the compass of a short poem. Although the poem begins and ends in the narrative past tense the language so creates a sense of immediate action – the implied physical movements of restless violence, the questions and exclamations, the arresting changes of tone – that one is drawn into this wrestling of a soul with itself. The effect comes near to that of dialogue, with one complaining voice characterized by a whining, pathetic note:

> What, shall I ever sigh and pine?
> My lines and life are free . . .

and ending with the almost despairing phrases, gasped out brokenly between sighs,

> all blasted?
> All wasted?

and the other, more vigorously rebellious voice, turning on the sighing heart with a decisive plan of action:

> Away! take heed;
> I will abroad.
> Call in thy death's-head there, tie up thy fears;
> He that forbears
> To suit and serve his need
> Deserves his load.

The conclusion seems at first sight (this is often the case with Herbert) a sudden and unprepared *volte-face*, like the surprising twist before a quick curtain. However, if we have taken in the submerged symbolism of Christ's loving sacrifice in the earlier, complaining lines

> (Have I no harvest but a thorn
> To let me blood, and not restore
> What I have lost with cordial fruit?)

we realize that what the poet has been trying to break free of is the claims of love, not the kinds of restraint which the rebellious voice has suggested. The action of the poem shows us the love of God working within the poet in spite of his distress and rebellion, and the conclusion is not a reversal but a consummation of the dramatic logic of the whole poem.

> But as I raved and grew more fierce and wild
>> At every word,
> Methought I heard one calling, 'Child';
>> And I replied, 'My Lord'.

The Collar enacts the resolution of dramatic tensions in a way which remains true to, and illuminates the nature of, the apparently disintegrating experience which it dramatizes.

Dialogue, an exchange between at least two characters, is necessary if drama is to create a more complex situation than Donne can achieve. Poems in dialogue do not necessarily take us further than Donne.

Ametas and Thestylis making Hay-Ropes

Ametas: Think'st thou that this love can stand,
　　　Whilst thou still dost say me nay?
　　Love unpaid does soon disband:
　　Love binds love as hay binds hay.

Thestylis: Think'st thou that this rope would twine
　　　If we both should turn one way?
　　Where both parties so combine,
　　Neither love will twist nor hay.

Ametas: Thus you vain excuses find,
　　Which yourself and us delay:
　　And love ties a woman's mind
　　Looser than with ropes of hay.

Thestylis: What you cannot constant hope
　　Must be taken as you may.

Ametas: Then let's both lay by our rope,
　　And go kiss within the hay.

Marvell's language is more relaxed than Donne's; the speakers inhabit the rarified world of pastoral convention. The poem has the seeds of drama in it. It portrays a relationship in which the shepherdess's arch coyness has finally misfired by making her lover more grumpy than ardent, and shows how she escapes from the impasse her behaviour has created, by first justifying herself (her first speech might be paraphrased: 'It takes the spice out of love if a girl says yes too quickly') and then wittily dropping it. Yet the effect is not dramatic, but reminds us rather, in its delicately poised wit, of an elegant and finely controlled dance, the feelings being kept within the limit of what can be gracefully expressed. It is a far cry from that to this:

> *Enter Macbeth.*
>
> *Lady Macbeth:*   My Husband!
> *Macbeth:*   I have done the deed. Didst thou not hear a noise?
> *Lady Macbeth:* I heard the owl scream and the crickets cry.
>   Did not you speak?
> *Macbeth:*   When?
> *Lady Macbeth:*   Now.
> *Macbeth:*   As I descended?
> *Lady Macbeth:* Ay.
> *Macbeth:*   Hark!
>   Who lies i' the second chamber?
> *Lady Macbeth:*   Donalbain.
> *Macbeth:*   This is a sorry sight.
> *Lady Macbeth:* A foolish thought to say a sorry sight.

Here every word seems to be compelled from the speakers despite a resistance, a reluctance to put into words what they are about which is expressed in Macbeth's 'the deed'. But as well as the tension of horror there is a tension which separates the two – Lady Macbeth's anxiety lest Macbeth (to put it in words quite inadequate to the situation) make a fool of himself. The noise that Macbeth asks about might have been a real noise, and therefore something to be concerned about. On the other hand it might have been the product of Macbeth's oversensitive and superstitious imagination, which she knows she must guard against. So the short exchanges give a sense of suppressed hysteria playing against the scornful matter-of-factness of Lady Macbeth's last speech.

All drama could not be conducted at this level of tension, but it is characteristic of dramatic dialogue at its best that each utterance seems to be called out by its predecessor in what is in one sense a kind of conflict (tension between characters) and in another a collaboration (clarifying the nature of the situation). The following exchange between Lorenzo, Bellimperia and Balthazar, from Kyd's *The Spanish Tragedy*, provides a striking contrast.

Lor: Sister, what means this melancholy walk?
Bel: That for a while I wish no company.
Lor: But here the prince is come to visit you.
Bel: That argues that he lives in liberty.
Bal: No, madam, but in pleasing servitude.
Bel: Your prison then, belike, is your conceit.
Bal: Ay, by conceit my freedom is enthralled.
Bel: Then with conceit enlarge yourself again.
Bal: What, if conceit have laid my heart to gage?
Bel: Pay that you borrowed, and recover it.
Bal: I die, if it return from whence it lies.
Bel: A heartless man and live? A miracle!
Bal: Ay, lady, love can work such miracles.
Lor: Tush, tush, my lord! let go these ambages,
      And in plain terms acquaint her with your love.

The clockwork effect of this *stichomythia* is not altogether a necessary result of the form itself; Shakespeare uses something like it in the striking passage between Richard and Anne in *Richard III*, Act I, Scene ii. One might say that it comes 'too pat', but what really condemns it is its rhythmical monotony. One has no impression of the thought actually forming itself during the course of the exchange, of a mind responding to the pressure of experience. It is a matter for argument how far the passage could be brought off by accomplished acting in a stylized production, but my own experience suggests that it presents considerable difficulties. Eric Bentley, in distinguishing between rhetoric and poetry in drama, makes use of D. W. Harding's characterization of the language of poetry.

> The rhetorician is rightly said to clothe thoughts in suitable words, and that is to imply that the thoughts already existed fully enough for us to judge that they are now *suitably* clothed. Now if they existed, they existed in words – presumably other words, and less suitable ones. Hence the rhetorician is an improver of phraseology . . . . The poet, on the other hand, likes – if I may paraphrase D. W. Harding – to get at a thought before it is fully a thought, before it has been pinned down with words. With him, the word-finding and the thought-thinking proceed together, and the result is, not necessarily new vocabulary, but new language, new phrasing, new combinations of vocabulary, new rhythms, new meaning.
>
> (*The Life of the Drama*, p. 90)

This poetic-dramatic language gives the audience or reader the sense of the thought being formed by the character as he speaks, under the pressure of the situation in which he finds himself.

II

Dramatic language, then, has force and immediacy. But its function is also to create the 'setting', the world within which the action takes place. In Donne's *The Sun Rising* this is achieved with careless economy:

> go chide
> Late school-boys and sour prentices,
> Go tell court-huntsmen that the King will ride,
> Call country ants to harvest offices. . . .

The world outside may be, as it often is in Donne, evoked merely to be dismissed, but it is nevertheless *there*, the context within which the lovers make of their love what they do make of it. This sense of a world of facts and concepts within which the dramatic situation develops, and in terms of which it is to be understood, is central to all drama, and it can of course be much more richly created when two or more speakers are involved. No single speech, however dramatic, could establish the atmosphere of tension and nervous expectancy of the opening pages of *Hamlet*. This is a passage so famous that comment may seem superfluous. However, it is worth noting how vital it is that Hamlet himself should not be present in this opening scene. These are ordinary men, some super-stitious, some sceptical, who naturally connect the appearance of a ghost with some public disaster ('This bodes some strange eruption to our state') and turn to a discussion of the latest political crisis. The ghost, that is, however strange, cannot concern them person-ally, cannot strike at their inner peace; they chat, in the manner of people telling ghost-stories, about folk-lore, omens and fairies. A world is already established in which Hamlet's ways of thinking and feeling are not the normal ways; to give one example, his horror and revulsion at his mother's marriage is not shared by the wider, if more commonplace, world which Barnardo and Marcellus inhabit. If we are not to surrender our vision entirely to Hamlet's we must remain aware of this world, and the claims that it makes.

The nature of a play's world determines what can happen within the play, limits the possible situations, the range or depth of the action. These limits are what critics of drama used to call 'decorum'. (See Note A, p. 85.) There are many different kinds of limitation. Confining the characters and their speech to a particular social class is one very obvious way of defining a world – Ibsen's plays belong to a middle-class world with skeletons in its cupboards, and a conviction that 'people don't do such things'. Yet we are often aware (in *The Wild Duck* for instance) of a wilder, more primitive world outside, the forests and mountains, and the legends that attach to them. Racine, on the other hand, creates a world of kings and princesses, of palaces and galleries, which seems as far as possibly removed from 'le fond des forêts'. Only gradually is it borne in on us that the civilization of the palaces and the dark wildness of the forests are not so far apart, and that the savagery of wild beasts and monsters is no more dangerous than that of a civilized human heart in the grip of irresistible passion. This contrast between surface and interior worlds is of great importance in drama; what separates Hamlet from everyone else is his acute sense of dimensions of human experience (heaven and hell, for instance) of which no one else in the play is aware. The whole world of a play is comprehended by no single character. This is the significance of the traditional idea expressed in 'All the world's a stage', or implied in the religious idea of the world as the theatre of God's judgement. *We*, as audience, are in a position to understand and to judge as none of the inhabitants of the created world can be. We see it all. And, as Suzanne Langer has expressed it, 'We do not have to find what is significant; the selection has been made – whatever is there is significant, and it is not too much to be surveyed *in toto*.'

III

When we categorize plays as comedies, tragedies, farces and so on we are, in fact, responding to the nature of the world the dramatist has created. The categories are of necessity rough and ready, taking little account of the variety possible within each 'kind'. The comic worlds of Shakespeare's *As You Like It*, Jonson's *The Alchemist* and Molière's *Le Misanthrope* (to choose three unquestioned masterpieces) differ widely. Jonson in particular has a narrow range within which he can operate at maximum intensity. The whole action of *The Alchemist* takes place within a single house, and the rich and varied life of the London outside has to be suggested by the language; the technique resembles Donne's in some ways. The opening scene is an object-lesson in dramatic economy. It is a quarrel-scene, the crude vigour of which expresses the unscrupulous dynamism of the three main characters, Subtle, Face and Doll. Here, we feel, is the energy which will keep things moving if the three rogues are able to work together according to their 'indenture tripartite', but will, if uncontrolled, destroy the whole undertaking. The outside world is quickly established as being there to be deceived:

> *Doll:*   Will you have
> The neighbours hear you? Will you betray all?
> Hark! I hear somebody.

To the danger of thieves falling out is added the danger of discovery, and the possible return of Face's master, whose house they are using.

> *Subtle:* Who's that? one rings. To the window Doll – pray heaven
> The master does not trouble us this quarter.

But what is chiefly striking in the language of the three is their grasp of the sheer physicality of things.

> When you went pinned up in the several rags
> You had raked and picked from dunghills, before day;
> Your feet in mouldy slippers for your kibes;
> A felt of rug, and a thin threadbare cloak
> That scarce would cover your no buttocks.

No other dramatist so fills his world with solid, tangible objects, a whole universe of things to be eaten, worn, fingered, enjoyed, bought and sold, or stolen. Jonson's is a world of energy and things, a tough world in which one either swindles or is swindled. Scruples, principles, sentiments, traditions or tender feelings which might get in the way of success are contemptuously ignored or swept aside. The only art is the art of dissimulation, the only science the science of hood-winking.

Jonson's world undoubtedly excludes enormous areas of human experience, but they are excluded deliberately; it would be missing the point to exclaim that life is not like that. Jonson is not making a mistake about life, he is creating a world in which certain limited aspects of life can be isolated and intensified. The monstrous figure of Sir Epicure Mammon is certainly an exaggeration, a caricature, but he is an exaggeration of certain human potentialities which are in all of us. Exclusion and intensification are of the essence of drama. The pastoral world of the Forest of Arden in *As You Like It* is no more the real world than Jonson's, and indeed one might say that in this play Shakespeare chooses to stress what Jonson leaves out. Here the greatest suffering is that of unrequited love, the worst failing that lack of intuitive sympathy with such suffering which Rosalind feigns with Orlando and diagnoses in Phebe. Molière's world, on the other hand, is pre-eminently social and elegant, even in the most intimate situations.

> Quoi! de mes sentiments l'obligeante assurance
> Contre tous vos soupçons ne prend pas ma défense?
> Auprès d'un tel garant sont-ils de quelque poids?
> N'est-ce pas m'outrager que d'écouter leurs voix?
> Et, puisque notre cœur fait un effort extrême
> Lorsqu'il peut se résoudre à confesser qu'il aime;
> Puisque l'honneur du sexe, ennemi de nos feux,
> S'oppose fortement à de pareils aveux,
> L'amant qui voit pour lui franchir un tel obstacle
> Doit-il impunément douter de cet oracle?
>
> (*Le Misanthrope*, Act IV, Scene iii)

(What! does not the kind assurance of my feelings for you take my defence against your own suspicions? Can those suspicions carry any weight against such a guarantee? Do you not insult me merely by listening to them? A woman's heart must overcome considerable resistance before resolving on a confession of love, since our sex's honour, enemy of our passions, opposes itself to such avowals. Can a lover who sees us overcome such an obstacle for his sake doubt with impunity what should be an oracle to him?)

Célimène here implies that the very artificialities of social life, with its polished surfaces and polite insincerities, constitute a guarantee that certain avowals must be sincere; one does not raise one's defences for trivial reasons. Molière was not incapable of seeing beyond the world of politeness and self-control which he creates, and obviously Alceste, in his detestation of the pretence which it necessitates, gains a great deal of sympathy. What he does show, however, is that Alceste's moral position, hostile as it is to some of the social necessities, nevertheless belongs within that society, a fact which only his monstrous egotism prevents him from seeing.

> Je vais sortir d'un gouffre où triomphent les vices,
> Et chercher sur la terre un endroit écarté
> Où d'être homme d'honneur on ait la liberté.

(I am getting out of an abyss where vice is triumphant, to search the earth for some remote spot where one has freedom to be a man of honour.)

How, Molière implicitly asks, can one be 'homme d'honneur' in a desert?

3
Action and Tension

The dramatist establishes the limits of the world which the play will inhabit. At the same time he seizes our attention by creating a situation which is interesting in itself, and which arouses expectation of further situations which may develop out of it. Thus, in the opening scene of *The Alchemist*, our attention is held by a quarrel in the course of which, with perfect naturalness, the situation defines itself. We become aware of short-term and long-term expectations; we are curious to see how these three, who can quarrel so uproariously, can employ their undoubted energy and eloquence in collaboration, while at the same time we wonder how long it will be before the disagreement breaks out again, the neighbours begin to suspect what is going on, or the master returns from the country. This is the potential which every dramatic situation contains, although to say 'we wonder' is misleading if the wondering is thought of as at all separate from our taking in what is happening at the moment. We do not contemplate the action, we are taken into it, hence our sense of what *is* happening is in fact indistinguishable from our sense of what *will* or *may* happen.

> This creates the peculiar tension between the given present and its yet unrealised consequent, 'form in suspense', the essential dramatic illusion. This illusion of a visible future is created in every play. . . . The future appears as already an entity, embryonic in the present.
>
> (Langer, op. cit., p. 311. See also Note B, p. 86)

'Tension' is a word which is bound to recur in any discussion of drama. We naturally speak of a 'tense situation' when we wish to convey the feeling that the state of affairs might at any moment be transformed into something crucially different. All works of art are fully grasped through the perception of the interrelatedness of their parts, and in drama the relation between parts is characteristically one of tension. In looking at two contrasting pictures, say a primitive madonna and an El Greco, we might distinguish them by saying that the latter was more dramatic. What we would mean is that the various elements in the picture – lines, spaces and colours – coexist in a state of tension, and seem perpetually on the verge of flying apart. It is no doubt useful to remember, as I. A. Richards reminds us in *The Principles of Literary Criticism,* that this tension is in us, but we can only discuss it in terms of the work of art itself, which is why psychological concepts like 'catharsis' can be so dangerously misleading. We may say of a play that it has us 'on the edge of our seats', but this is not in itself a critical comment.

There are many different kinds of tension in drama – between different ways in which a speech may be understood (dramatic irony), between two characters, and so on – but the underlying, continuous tension is that between the situation at any given moment and the complete action. A play remains in a state of imperfect equilibrium until the completion of the action, and the most simple and striking example of this tension is suspense. We can see this most clearly at the level of popular dramatic entertainment in films and television. The heroine is tied to the railway lines: cut to the express train, hugely powerful and menacingly mindless, eating up the last few miles: cut to the hero on his white horse, galloping desperately to the rescue. Melodrama is merely drama reduced to its simplest terms – the darkening main street of a western township, from each end of which emerges a solitary figure, hands poised nervously over holsters. The great master of popular entertainment, a Chaplin or a Hitchcock, has an instinctive knowledge (which is a kind of genius) just how long the tension can be maintained without becoming either unbearable or tedious, and how it can be broken with maximum effect.

Suspense, often taking very subtle forms, is inseparable from drama. Chehov is the master of unresolved or partially resolved suspense, and Ibsen relies on it for some of his most powerful scenes, like the conclusion of *The Master Builder*. It often takes the form of a crucial decision that has to be made, like Corneille's choice between love and duty. All farce creates suspense, of the kind we experience when a juggler continues to add to the number of balls he is keeping in the air simultaneously; *The Alchemist* is probably the most brilliant example. One of the most superbly suspenseful scenes in all drama is Act IV, Scene v of Molière's *Le Tartuffe*. Tartuffe, the 'faux devôt', has been making advances to the wife of his patron, the besotted Orgon, but Orgon refuses to believe it. Elmire, the wife, arranges for him to hide under the table during an interview between herself and Tartuffe. Elmire, in her determination to lead Tartuffe to a point where his intentions are most scandalously apparent, finds herself trapped when her husband, despite her increasingly frantic signalling by coughs and rappings on the table, does not leap out to confront Tartuffe. When she finally gets rid of him for a moment (ironically to see whether Orgon is likely to discover them) she turns sarcastically on her husband, who has emerged from under the table:

> Quoi! vous sortez sitôt? Vous vous moquez des gens.
> Rentrez sous le tapis, il n'est pas encore temps;
> Attendez jusqu'au bout, pour voir les choses sûres,
> Et ne vous fiez point aux simples conjectures.

(What! come out so soon? You can't be serious! get back under the tablecloth, it's not time yet. You must wait until the end in order to be quite certain, and not rely on mere conjecture.)

The comedy, however, is not entirely at the expense of Orgon, for Elmire, in her rather facile self-confidence, has created a situation in which she is brought face to face with an unscrupulous force against which she alone is defenceless. The scene ends with the re-establishment of trust between husband and wife, but it has demonstrated, by means of suspense, how near Tartuffe had come to destroying completely the mutual respect on which marriage rests.

Another simple means of creating dramatic tension is surprise, the sudden introduction of a new element into an established situation, so as to immediately transform it. Here again the most obvious examples are melodramatic, like the sudden revelation of an important fact of which we have been kept in ignorance. Effects of this kind are common and dangerously easy – the pistol-shot off-stage, the unexpected entrance – and we can find striking examples in Ibsen, such as the suicide of Hedda Gabler, or the appearance of Mrs Borkman at the end of Act II of *John Gabriel Borkman*. (Ibsen, despite the naturalism of his settings and language, is rarely far removed from melodrama.)

At this point, however, it becomes necessary to recognize that the foregoing account of suspense and surprise is over-simplified. There may be in drama cases where the surprise is complete, there may be cases of suspense in which we are entirely uncertain of the outcome. But even in the melodramatic instances we are rarely entirely ignorant or entirely uncertain. We know, in fact, when we are watching a 'cliff-hanger', that the hero and heroine will survive; we have usually been to some extent prepared for the possibility of the surprise. Our sense of the probabilities has its origin in our knowledge of the conventions of the particular type of drama. Thus, in the scene from *Le Tartuffe* already described, we know 'at the back of our minds' that Tartuffe will not succeed in seducing Elmire. This is partly because we can be sure (or could until quite recently) that the seduction could not be presented on stage; what can and cannot be shown on stage may be a matter of fashion or public taste, but it nevertheless sets limits on our dramatic expectations. But primarily it is a matter of decorum, of what can properly be expected in this sort of play, and this the play has established from the very beginning of the action.

The range of possibilities has never been narrower than it was in Greek tragedy, in which the story was almost invariably a legend known to the entire audience. Anyone who believes that dramatic suspense depends on literal ignorance of the outcome would be well advised to read Sophocles' *King Oedipus*, and observe the way in which the tension develops between the ignorance of all the characters (with the exception of Tiresias, who has left the stage before the truth begins to emerge), an ignorance we 'share' through our identification with the characters, and our knowledge of what the truth really is. The nature of this 'double consciousness', as one might call it, will be examined more closely in the following chapter, in the discussion of irony.

Shakespeare rarely if ever creates situations of simple suspense, and very rarely uses surprise. Even the most strikingly dramatic moments in the tragedies, like the appearance of Banquo's ghost or the entrance of Lear with the dead Cordelia in his arms, we have been half prepared for, so that when they happen they strike us immediately as being perfectly right. Even on the one notable occasion when Shakespeare does keep something from us, the preservation of Hermione in *The Winter's Tale*, we find that her reappearance has been almost imperceptibly prepared for by the preceding scenes, in the references to her and the whole atmosphere of rediscovered joy and love.

This is the supreme art of the dramatist, the creation of an underlying sense of what the action must be, which does not emerge into full consciousness until the action is at last completed, so that there is a perpetual tension between this, and what is happening at any particular moment. The conclusion of the play, an analogy with music being most appropriate here, is like the final major chord of a symphony which has throughout been there *in potentia*, which we never actually hear until the end, and which sets the seal on our intuitive understanding of what has gone before.

II

We can be taken into the initial situation of a play in very different ways. There is, for instance, the sudden, violent or noisy beginning, like that of *Romeo and Juliet*. Here we encounter another necessary condition of a complete action, the focusing of our attention on what is central to the situation. In terms of the action of *Romeo and Juliet* it is the feud, and not the individuals involved, which has to be established. Therefore Shakespeare begins with the servants. It is a commonplace but nevertheless useful observation that there are certain advantages to a dramatist in portraying a society in which social gradations are clear and quickly discerned. No one is likely to be misled into thinking that the play is going to be about Sampson and Gregory, because they are servants. The characters of any play are subject to an implicit scheme of subordination, and nothing is more frustrating to an audience than being allowed to mistake where the centre of interest lies. Webster, for instance, begins *The White Devil* in a fine, explosive manner.

> *Lodovico:* Banished?
> *Antonelli:* It grieved me much to hear the sentence.
> *Lodovico:* Ha, ha, O Democritus, thy gods
> That govern the whole world! – Courtly reward
> And punishment! Fortune's a right whore:
> If she give aught, she deals it in small parcels,
> That she may take away all at one swoop.
> This 'tis to have great enemies, God 'quite them:
> Your wolf no longer seems to be a wolf
> Than when she's hungry.

The speech itself is of considerable dramatic importance, for the idea of 'courtly reward/ And punishment' and 'great enemies' is central to the ensuing action. But Lodovico himself, after this opening scene, virtually disappears until near the end of Act III, and his degree of involvement in the later action is not particularly plausible. It is notorious that Webster's 'dramatic structure' is often at fault, but this particular example may help us to see more clearly what dramatic structure *is*. The phrase itself has its dangers; with its implicit comparison with physical structures it encourages critics to draw graphs and diagrams. We can save ourselves from this by taking account once more of the importance of attention, for what we call dramatic structure is the means whereby what is most important in the action is kept consistently in the centre of our attention. (See Note C, p. 89.)

A concern with structure in this sense lies behind most of the so-called 'neo-classical' rules of drama, such as the unities, and the condemnation of double actions and the mixture of tragic and comic scenes. Johnson's defence of Shakespeare from neo-classical strictures (in his *Preface*) often amounts to saying that life itself does not admit such limitations, and that drama is a mirror of life. But it is no *artistic* defence of the porter in *Macbeth* or the fool in *Lear*, both of whom do, in effect, point our attention firmly in the right direction. We do not emerge from a performance of *Macbeth* saying, 'I wonder what happened to that porter?' The fool in *Lear* is not such a simple matter, but the interesting question here is not, 'What happened to the fool?' but whether in asking such a question we are either misunderstanding his role in the action or drawing attention to a flaw in the play's structure. (It may usefully be noted here that this last problem, if it is a problem, is related to the difficulties many critics have experienced with Shylock in *The Merchant of Venice*, or Malvolio in *Twelfth Night*. Here the difficulty is not so much the amount of attention as the kind of attention which the two characters have attracted, but the cases serve to remind us of the extent to which character and structure are related.)

When we talk of dramatic structure we are making an abstraction from the way in which situations are related one to another, and from the way in which our attention is focused on those situations so as to unify them into an action. 'Whose fate are we most particularly concerned to follow?' is one of the first questions posed by the opening scenes of a play. There are some plays in which only one or two characters really matter – the main plot of *The Changeling* springs to mind, and there is the obvious case of the tragedies of Aeschylus and Sophocles. Chehov, pre-eminently among the great dramatists, presents difficulties. If we ask ourselves the question I have formulated above we are likely to be puzzled. There is a sense in which, in *The Cherry Orchard*, some of the characters are more important than others (the governess Charlotta, for instance, is less important than her mistress Liubov Andreyeevna or her charge Ania) but the lesser characters do not serve primarily to direct attention to what is most important or significant in the major characters. They belong to their own situations, which, like those of the major characters, point our attention towards – what? '*What* fate are we most particularly concerned to follow?' would be a better way of putting it, for it allows us to reply – 'The cherry orchard', the past and present of a social order which has no future, just as the relationships of which we see the potential (Varia and Lopahin, Ania and Trofimov) have no future. Chehov's is the drama of characters who have no destiny; its spirit is best summed up in the closing lines of *The Three Sisters*.

> *Olga:* . . . . No, my dear sisters, life isn't finished for us yet! We're going to live! The band is playing so cheerfully and joyfully – maybe, if we wait a little longer, we shall find out why we live, why we suffer. . . . Oh, if only we knew, if only we knew!
>
> *Chebutykin (sings quietly to himself):* Tarara-boom-di-ay . . . I'm sitting on a tomb-di-ay. . . . (*Reads the paper.*) What does it matter? Nothing matters.
>
> *Olga:* If only we knew, if only we knew! . . .

Does not Chehov, in these two great plays, at once anticipate and surpass the whole of the modern so-called 'theatre of the absurd'?

III

The opening scenes of a play are of paramount importance, since they define the situation from which the whole action will grow, and establish the central concerns of the play by focusing our attention. But if we take a play like *King Lear* or *The Master Builder*, it is obvious that, while the opening points unmistakably to the centre of interest (Lear, Solness) the nature of that interest is not clearly defined, and cannot be fully understood until the end of the action. For as one situation grows out of another, so the new situation points to something in the old which we would not other-wise have seen. In Act I, Scene iii of *King Lear*, Goneril, referring to the king, remarks:

> Old fools are babes again, and must be used
> With checks as flatteries when they are seen abused.

Lear, as the fool is later to reiterate, has placed himself in the position of his daughters' child, and is thus necessarily subject to their authority. But this, as we realize on returning to the opening scene, is precisely the situation he wished to be in *vis-à-vis* Cordelia, and which Cordelia, by refusing to humour him, rendered impossible.

> (I loved her most, and thought to set my rest
> On her kind nursery.)

But this is to open the whole question of dramatic irony, which requires a separate chapter.

4
Dramatic Irony

We most commonly think of irony as a tone of voice. 'It is a truth universally acknowledged that a single man in possession of a good fortune must be in want of a wife.' This, the opening sentence of *Pride and Prejudice*, is probably one of the best-known examples of irony in the language. Like all irony it moves, as it were, in several different directions simultaneously. To begin with, there is in fact a strong probability that a 'single man in possession of a good fortune' *will* be in want of a wife. But the weighty generality of 'a truth universally acknowledged' puts us on our guard, makes us aware, in stimulating our critical sense, that this is not a universal truth (there are exceptions to it) and makes us aware of the probable limitations of those who, like Mrs Bennet, could not be brought to admit that there may be exceptions. The irony establishes common ground between Jane Austen and the reader, which will never be entirely shared even by her most sympathetic characters. A dramatic situation is established by the irony, but it is established by means of tone, and tone is a resource which is necessarily unavailable to the dramatist. The novelist can avail himself of the many infinitely subtle gradations between the direct address to the reader and the fully dramatic presentation in which the narrator as such may be said to withdraw himself completely from the action. The dramatist, *as* dramatist, cannot.

There are, of course, a number of different ways in which the dramatist can attempt to get round this difficulty, with prologues, epilogues, the use of a chorus and so on, but these means are of

necessity incidental to drama. He can certainly put ironical language into the mouth of one of his characters, like Lady Macbeth's
famous

> He that's coming
> Must be provided for.

This is deliberate irony, understood as such by the speaker and her
husband. But there is a further, dramatic irony in the full force of
the savage pun. For Lady Macbeth, immediately before her husband's entrance, has invoked the spirits of evil to 'unsex me here'.
The full force of the contrast between providing for an expected
guest (in the humble terms of bedding, food and other entertainment) which would normally be the woman's responsibility, and
making provision for an inhuman murder, lies in the extent to
which Lady Macbeth has succeeded in throwing off the normal
feminine role.

> Come, thick night,
> And pall thee in the dunnest smoke of hell,
> That my keen knife see not the wound it makes,
> Nor heaven peep through the blanket of the dark,
> To cry 'Hold, hold!'

Johnson, in commenting on this passage (*Rambler*, 168) takes
exception to what he calls the 'lowness' of words like 'knife' and
'blanket'. But Johnson attributes the speech to Macbeth, not his
wife, and thus misses the terrible irony of her use of words which
belong to the humble normality of preparing food and beds for an
expected guest.

It might be objected that this is a particularly subtle example,
which would hardly be observed in performance. This is an objection commonly raised to detailed interpretation of drama, but it is
fundamentally misconceived. Probably no one who did not know
the play well would be conscious of this irony, but dramatic poetry
can often, in T. S. Eliot's phrase, 'communicate before it is understood'. Detailed analysis of this kind does not aim merely at

expressing what can be consciously grasped in the theatre at first hearing, but at making conscious and explicit connections which would otherwise be obscurely felt as part of the 'rightness' of a general impression. Again and again in re-reading the great dramatists, and Shakespeare in particular, one experiences the delight of being able to explain to oneself for the first time exactly *why* a particular phrase or speech is just right for the character or the situation.

Most of the ironies of drama are by no means so subtle. They arise immediately the audience is aware of something of which at least one character on stage is ignorant. For we, the audience know all – we delight in our god-like omniscience, and this exhilaration reaches its height in comedy. Consider, for instance, the central situation in Goldsmith's charming *She Stoops to Conquer*. Young Marlowe, on his way to visit for the first time his father's friend Mr Hardcastle, is persuaded that Mr Hardcastle's house is an inn. He therefore behaves as he naturally would at an inn, greatly to Mr Hardcastle's astonishment. The joke is made richer by the fact that Marlow has been described to Mr Hardcastle as an extremely diffident young man. Everything said and done in the house, up to Mr Hardcastle's discovery of his guest's mistake, is referred by the audience to its knowledge of the true situation. This is the simplest possible kind of dramatic irony, but in a sense all other kinds are an extension and deepening of this.

Comedy depends for the most part on mistakes or misunderstandings which are human and possible, mistakes *we* might have made; our sense of common humanity with the characters prevents our amusement from being merely detached and heartless. Thus, no one could take the full flavour of Goldsmith's comedy who was incapable of imagining what a fool he would feel if he made the same mistake. On the other hand, to feel this too acutely would be to spoil the fun in a different way; young children are often upset by plays which amuse their elders because they sympathize too deeply with the fate of a particular character. Different kinds of comedy strike a different balance between sympathy and detachment, and some dramatists deliberately inhibit the sympathetic response as much as possible. Among the classic dramatists one thinks of Ben Jonson, while in the modern theatre a great deal of so-called 'black' comedy and 'theatre of the absurd' is of this type. Bertold Brecht did indeed attempt to exclude sympathy entirely, though his instinctive dramatic gift happily prevented him from succeeding. For drama can exist only at some point between the two poles of complete sympathetic identification and complete detachment.

The full flavour of the situation in *She Stoops to Conquer* derives from the ignorance of both Young Marlowe and Mr Hardcastle. But there is another kind of irony which derives from our complicity or shared knowledge with one of the characters at the expense of others. This is often the case with that 'stock' character of comedy, the ingenious and intriguing rogue. The question is sometimes asked, how we can, as audience, delight in behaviour of which, by our normal standards, we would heartily disapprove. For all dramatic identification is not sympathetic in the way outlined above. In romantic comedy we naturally sympathize with the lovers; but we could hardly be said to *sympathize* with the amoral rogues of Ben Jonson and other Jacobean dramatists. Rather we are drawn by them into a complicity of shared knowledge, and become, in a sense, their accomplices, for as long as the dramatist inhibits any tendency on our part to sympathize with the dupes. (This might be compared with the satisfaction one might feel at being 'let in on' a joke being practised on someone who has alienated our sympathy, and no doubt the psychologists would have something to say about the harmless satisfaction of aggressive impulses.)

This irony of complicity is common in Elizabethan and Jacobean drama, and in Shakespearian comedy is often achieved by means of disguises and concealments. A particularly rich example occurs in *As You Like It*. Rosalind loves Orlando, and he loves her, but when they meet in the Forest of Arden she is disguised as a boy. To the question why she does not reveal her identity immediately the answer might be given that one does not ask that kind of question about this kind of play. But there is more to it than that, for there are certain satisfactions which the situation can yield to Rosalind, such as the pleasure of hearing her lover confess his love to a 'third party'. She can *be* the third party, pour scorn on his protestations, and hear them redoubled in the face of that scorn.

> *Orlando:* Fair youth, I would I could make thee believe I love.
> *Rosalind:* Me believe it! You may as soon make her that you love believe it; which, I warrant, she is apter to do than to confess she does. That is one of the points in the which women still give the lie to their consciences. But, in good sooth, are you he that hangs the verses on the trees wherein Rosalind is so admired?
> *Orlando:* I swear to thee, youth, by the white hand of Rosalind, I am that he, that unfortunate he.
> *Rosalind:* But are you so much in love as your rhymes speak?
> *Orlando:* Neither rhyme nor reason can express how much.
> *Rosalind:* Love is merely a madness; and, I tell you, deserves as well a dark house and a whip as madmen do; and the reason why they are not so punished and cured is that the lunacy is so ordinary that the whippers are in love too.
>
> (Act I, Scene ii)

At this point in the scene Rosalind and the audience are almost at one in their contemplation of the irrationality of love, but the closing speech reminds us that this 'whipper' of love is in love, is part of the action as well as a member of the audience, and that we, as audience, are by virtue of our common humanity implicated in the 'madness' of love. Her pretence of being a detached observer is merely a teasing game, and we can only grasp the significance of the game if we remember that she is in love with the man she is addressing. The complex situation has an effect analogous with that of metaphysical 'wit'.

II

I have written of the delight and exhilaration we experience in the irony of comedy – the pleasure we take in knowing or understanding more than the *dramatis personae*. But what of tragedy? Our appreciation of tragic irony cannot be entirely different; the difference lies in what it is we understand. It would be generally agreed that tragedy produces a sense of foreboding, the intuition of a destiny quite other than the happy resolution of comedy, which might without exaggeration be called prophetic. It is not a foreknowledge of any particular outcome. (When the Ghost informs Hamlet that he was murdered by Claudius, Hamlet exclaims, 'O my prophetic soul!/ My uncle!' He does not mean by this that he has specifically suspected his uncle of having murdered his father, but rather that the revelation, as one might say, 'fits'.) Indeed, the precise form which tragic foreboding is likely to take at first is often misleading. In *Hamlet* itself the apprehensions of Horatio and his friends are not fulfilled – the 'state' in the political sense is well-conducted to the end of the play, and that which is 'rotten in the state of Denmark' is only gradually made clear by the developing action. Similarly, the witches in *Macbeth*, though obviously portentous of evil, do not point to the true evil of the play, the evil of the human heart, but rather, in their emergence as rather cheap and theatrical fortune-tellers, produce a near-comic contrast with it. Lady Macbeth's invocation of the spirits of evil is far more terrifying than the *Grand Guignol* list of ingredients for the witches' brew, or the tale of the sailor's wife and her chestnuts. The forebodings of the chorus in a Greek tragedy, *Agamemnon* for instance, are vague and confused. Turning to Ibsen we find that in *The Master Builder* (Act I) Solness expresses to Dr Herdal his fear of youth 'knocking at the door' in the person of his draughts-man, who is ambitious to set up on his own in competition with Solness. Almost immediately there is a knock at the door, and Hilde Wangel enters and introduces herself. Dr Herdal makes a joke of it.

> *Herdal:* ... You made a true prophecy, after all, Mr Solness!
> *Solness:* How did I?
> *Herdal:* The younger generation *did* come and knock at your door.
> *Solness (cheerfully):* Ah well, that was in quite a different way.

Yet it is youth in the person of Hilde, not the young draughtsman, which destroys Solness.

It is by such ironic contrasts as this that the forebodings of tragedy are gradually brought into sharper focus as the action develops and its significance emerges. For the action is the gradual unfolding of the meaning of the initial situation. This is strikingly true of a great tragedy like *King Lear*, in which almost every speech and action fills out the significance of the two opening scenes, makes explicit what was already implicit. This gradual unfolding of the true nature of a situation is in some ways like the classic accounts of the process of psychoanalysis, in which the symptoms (anxiety for instance) are, as the result of a process analogous to drama, eventually recognized in their true signifi-cance. When the subject is brought to the point where he recog-nizes this significance, what he acknowledges is the conclusion of a complete and satisfying action. He has been brought to this recognition in a manner prophetically recommended by Edgar in the closing lines of *King Lear*:

> Speak what we feel, not what we ought to say.

5
Character and Idea

I

It is impossible to write about characters in drama without recognizing the kind of questions about the usefulness of the concept which have been raised in this century, in particular by critics of Shakespeare. It may be useful at this point to adduce two contrasting passages as evidence.

> Why did [Iago] act as we see him acting in the play? What is the answer to that appeal of Othello's:
>
> > Will you, I pray, demand that demi-devil
> > Why he hath thus ensnared my soul and body?
>
> This question Why? is *the* question about Iago, just as the question Why did Hamlet delay? is *the* question about Hamlet. Iago refuses to answer it; but I will venture to say that he *could* not have answered it, any more than Hamlet could tell why he delayed. But Shakespeare knew the answer, and if these characters are great creations and not blunders we ought to be able to find it out too.
>
> (A. C. Bradley, *Shakespearean Tragedy*, paperback edn, London, 1965, p. 181)

And finally, as to 'character'. In the following essays the term is refused, since it is so constantly entwined with a false and unduly ethical criticism. . . . It continually brings in the intention-concept, which our moral-philosophy, rightly or wrongly, involves. Hence, too, the constant and fruitless search for 'motives' sufficient to account for Macbeth's and Iago's actions. . . . Thus when a critic adopts the ethical attitude, we shall generally find that he is unconsciously lifting the object of his attention from his setting and regarding him as actually alive.

(G. Wilson Knight, *The Wheel of Fire*, University Paperbacks, London., 1960, pp. 9–11)

L. C. Knights, in his essay. 'How Many Children Had Lady Macbeth?' (in *Explorations*, Peregrine, Harmondsworth, 1964, pp. 13–50) traces the development of the character analysis approach to Shakespeare to a number of eighteenth-century critics.

The reader must be sensible of something in the composition of *Shakespeare's* characters, which renders them essentially different from those drawn by other writers . . . there is a certain roundness and integrity in the forms of *Shakespeare*, which give them an independence as well as a relation. . . . The reader will not now be surprised if I affirm that those characters in Shakespeare, which are seen only in part, are yet capable of being unfolded and understood in the whole; every part being in fact relative, and inferring all the rest. . . . A felt propriety and truth from causes unseen, I take to be the highest point of Poetic composition. If the characters of *Shakespeare* are thus *whole* and as it were original, whilst those of almost all other writers are mere imitation, it may be fit to consider them rather as Historic than Dramatic beings; and, when occasion requires, to account for their conduct from the *whole* of character, from general principles, from latent motives, and from policies not avowed.

(Maurice Morgann, *Essay on the Dramatic Character of Sir John Falstaff*, 1777)

What is admirable about this passage is Morgann's absolute clarity about what he is doing. As a general prescription it is positively misleading, but we can see clearly where the danger lies. Morgann's method is akin to that of the historical novelist who attempts to illuminate what actually *did* happen (the text of the play standing in the place of the historical evidence) by imagining what *might* have happened. Because it is a method fraught with possibilities of distortion and irrelevance, must we therefore say that it cannot, by its nature, throw a revealing light on the play as it stands? In the end it is the quality of the imagination and intelligence of the critic that is in question, not his *method*. Every 'approach' to Shakespeare which can be formulated as a *modus operandi* has its dangers, and it will remain a matter for argument in specific cases how far a commitment to a given approach has distorted a critic's account of any play, and this applies as much to a concern with iterative imagery or 'themes' as to a preoccupation with character.

What we can safely say is that in some plays there are some characters who, in Morgann's phrase, have 'a certain roundness and integrity' which invites psychological explanation, and the kind of inference which Morgann recommends. These are what Eric Bentley, in a stimulating discussion of the whole matter, calls 'mysterious' characters.

> The 'great' characters – Hamlet, Phaedra, Faust, Don Juan – have something enigmatic about them. In this they stand in stark and solemn contrast to – for example – the people of the present-day psychological play who are fully *explained*. The effect of such a modern play is of a naïve rationalism: reason has either explained everything, or is in the process of doing so, and a cast of characters is at best a row of extinct volcanoes. The enigmatic nature of great characters also carries a cosmic implication: that life is but a small light in the midst of a vast darkness.

> > We are such stuff
> > As dreams are made on, and our little life
> > Is rounded with a sleep.

> The lines are so familiar, we forget that they may, or even must, be taken as the final conclusion of the greatest of playwrights on his principal subjects: human beings. How true, in any event, these words are of human beings in the plays of William Shakespeare! How faithfully they represent the life of the plays – so luminous at the centre yet shading off toward the edges into a metaphysical mystery. . . .

If the final effect of greatness in dramatic characterization is one of mystery, we see, once again, how bad it is for us, the audience, to demand or expect that all characters should be either predefined abstract types or newly defined concrete individuals. A mysterious character is one with an open definition – not completely open, or there will be no character at all, and the mystery will dwindle to a muddle, but open as, say, a circle is open when most of the circumference has been drawn. Hamlet might be called an accepted instance of such a character, for, if not, what have all those critics been doing, with their perpetual redefining of him? They have been closing the circle which Shakespeare left open. Which is not foolish, but very likely what Shakespeare intended. Foolish are only those critics who assume that the great geometrician would leave a circle open by accident.

(op. cit., pp. 68–9)

What Mr Bentley calls the 'mystery' of a great dramatic character is precisely what drives a critic like Bradley to ask Why? but the answers to questions of this kind will always belong within a conceptual scheme of psychology or ethics by which the critic himself is limited. *Some* light will perhaps be shed on the play, as, for instance, by Freudian interpretations of *Hamlet*, in so far as the critic has directed our attention towards something in the play which we might otherwise have missed. But there are two objections to the approach: firstly, that it easily becomes a kind of 'substitute creation', in which the critic virtually rewrites the play to fit into his own conceptual scheme; and secondly, that it runs the risk of ignoring the poetic-dramatic function of characters, and the fact that much of the language of a play points beyond character, ironically, towards the whole action and its significance.

There is a further objection to be raised against character-analysis, on the grounds of dramatic convention, decorum and structure. Most characters in most plays do not in fact repay that kind of attention. Psychology is a by-product of drama, not the true life of it, and most characters are essentially *types* whose motivation is clear and unambiguous. We can see this at its simplest in morality plays such as *Everyman*. To ask, for instance, why Goods turns on Everyman in the way he does is not to require an analysis of Goods' motives. What we have to do is to understand the place which possessions have in the life of man. But since this is drama the understanding is not of a general or abstract kind – it has the particularity of life.

> *Goods:* What! weenest thou that I am thine?
> *Everyman:* I had weened so.
> *Goods:* Nay Everyman, I say no.
>   As for a while I was lent thee;
>   A season thou hast had me in prosperity.
>   My condition is man's soul to kill;
>   If I save one, a thousand I do spill.
>   Weenest thou that I will follow thee
>   From this world? nay, verily.
> *Everyman:* I had weened otherwise.
> *Goods:* Therefore to thy soul Good is a thief,
>   For when thou art dead, this is my guise,
>   Another to deceive in this same wise
>   As I have done thee, and all to his soul's reproof.

This is the voice of exhilarated malevolence, a human voice, not an abstraction, and in characterizing it as such we are referring to the feeling and attitude expressed in the language, which is appropriate to the role of Goods in the entire action. Goods is a *type*, and as far back as we can go in the history of drama we find, in Greek and Latin drama, in the Commedia dell' Arte and beyond, a common fund of traditional types, some of which remain essentially unchanged. The young lover, the old miser, the jealous husband, the intriguing servant, the blustering soldier, the ageing beauty, the pedantic official; from this common stock all the great dramatists have drawn. In some periods a type becomes particularly fashionable, like the revenger in Jacobean drama, or the fop in Restoration comedy. Sometimes dramatic types are created by current modes of psychological or social explanation, like the modern mother-fixated son, or the 'rebel without a cause', though even these are not so new as they seem, and the rebel without a cause appears as little more than the Jacobean 'malcontent' in blue jeans.

Stock characters may, of course, be described as dramatic clichés, in contrast with those characters who have undeniable individuality. Certainly we remember with particular vividness not categories or types, but individuals. Yet we find that these 'individuals' are often variations on a basic type, and are driven to ask whence springs this sense of individuality. What is it to create character?

One is tempted to reply that whatever it is it is not very difficult. If we consider the characters in any successful television series, and the way in which the audience responds to their changing fortunes as if they were real people, it becomes clear that within a coherent and recognizable setting a dramatic type can, with a few individual touches of speech, dress and manner contributed by the actor or actress, become virtually a national figure. Many an indifferent play has been rescued by an actor giving to a meagre and lifeless part his own vigour and individuality. But the significant life of a dramatic character is independent of any particular performance, of any identifiable physical presence. It is in the language of the play, and the situations which that language creates. The individuality of a Falstaff, a Polonius or a Malvolio is created by the speech put into his mouth, and into the mouths of those who speak to him and about him. It is typicality individualized by language which creates the impression we call character. Molière's Harpagon in *L'Avare* originates in the traditional stock figure of the miser, and the play is in fact an adaptation of Plautus' Latin comedy *Aulularia*. Even the great scene (Act IV, Scene vii) in which Harpagon bewails the theft of his money is based upon a similar scene in

Plautus. (See for comparison *The Pot of Gold*, p. 37, in *The Pot of Gold and other plays*, translated by E. F. Watling, Harmondsworth, 1965.) The life of the character is the life of the language.

Au voleur! au voleur! à l'assassin! au meurtrier! Justice, juste ciel! je suis perdu, je suis assassiné! on m'a coupé la gorge: on m'a dérobé mon argent! Qui peut-ce être? Qu'est-il devenu? Où est-il? Où se cache-t-il? Que ferai-je pour le trouver? Où courir? Où ne pas courir? N'est-il point là? N'est-il pas ici? Qui est-ce? Arrête! (*Il se prend lui-même par le bras.*) Rends-moi mon argent, coquin!. . . . Ah! c'est moi! Mon esprit est troublé, et j'ignore où je suis, qui je suis, et ce que je fais. Hélas, mon pauvre argent! mon cher ami! on m'a privé de toi; et, puisque tu m'es enlevé, j'ai perdu mon support, ma consolation, ma joie: tout est fini pour moi, et je n'ai plus que faire au monde. Sans toi, il m'est impossible de vivre. C'en est fait; je n'en puis plus; je me meurs; je suis mort; je suis enterré!. . . . Quel bruit fait-on là-haut? Est-ce mon voleur qui y est? De grâce, si l'on sait des nouvelles de mon voleur, je supplie que l'on m'en dise. N'est-il point caché là parmi vous? Ils me regardent tous et se mettent à rire. Vous verrez qu'ils ont part, sans doute, au vol que l'on m'a fait. Allons vite, des commissaires, des archers, des prévôts, des juges, des gênes, des potences, et des bourreaux. Je veux pendre tout le monde; et, si je ne retrouve mon argent, je me pendrai moi-même après. . . .

(Stop thief! stop thief! assassin! murderer! Justice, just heaven! I am lost, I am murdered, my throat has been cut: my money has been stolen! Who can it be? What has become of him? Where is he? Where is he hiding? How shall I find him? Where shall I run? Where shall I not run? Isn't he there? Isn't he here? Who is this? Halt! (*He takes hold of his own arm.*) Give me my money back, you rogue!. . . . Oh, it's me! My mind is troubled, I don't know where I am, who I am or what I am doing. Alas, my poor money! my poor money! my dear friend! they have taken you away from me; you raised me, and now I have lost my support, my consolation, my joy: it's all up with me, I no longer have anything to do in this world. I cannot live without you. That's it, then; I can't live any longer; I'm dying, I'm dead, I'm buried. . . . What's that noise out there? Is it my thief? I beg you, please, if anyone can give me news of my thief, speak up. He's hidden among you out there, isn't he? They all look at me and burst out laughing. You'll see, they are undoubtedly accomplices in the theft. Come quickly, superintendants, constables, provosts, judges, tortures, gallows, hangmen. I will hang the lot of them, and if I don't get my money back, I'll end up by hanging myself.)

What most impresses one about this passage is the way in which it enacts a state of mind, with its restless spasmodic vigour at the beginning, the onset of delirium as he arrests himself (literally a state of ecstasy) the plaintive tones of bereavement, and finally the force with which one is carried into Harpagon's hallucination, so that one is simultaneously with him in his agony and one of the audience who, in the theatre, actually constitute the hallucination itself, laughing at the absurdity of his anguish. The type has been invested with an individual life; it is the combination of the typical with the individual which makes this a great and memorable scene.

It is worth noting also how this scene brings out, in the way it simultaneously takes us into and makes us observers of Harpagon's plight, the tension between the 'inside' and the 'outside' of a situation which carries over into any discussion of character. A more complex example can be found in Act III of Ibsen's *John Gabriel Borkman*, when Erhart Borkman has claims made upon him by, in succession, his aunt, his mother and his father. As each of them pleads with him we momentarily identify ourselves with the point of view, we feel the strength of the claim. At the same time we are standing back and judging the situation, and the selfishness with which each of them asks him to make himself an extension of their own selves. Anything we say about any one of these three, as a character, will be the product of the tension between identification and judgement. Our knowledge of the whole situation is completed by the entrance of Mrs Wilton, confirming our suspicion (the revelation has been prepared for in preceding scenes) that Erhart has chosen already. This final touch, the realization by the three that Erhart is not the free agent they have taken him to be, takes us back once more into their sense of the situation, investing them with a further degree of pathos.

II

This tension between the inside and outside of a situation is, of course, productive of irony, and much of a dramatist's creation of character is intrinsically ironic. By being shown a character in different situations, displaying, as it were, different sides of himself, we are enabled to build up the impression of a complex whole. The Iago whom we hear advising Roderigo is the same man who jests with Desdemona and Emilia, and who deceives Othello. The dramatist does not explain his characters – he leaves his audience to make sense of what they say and do, and different individuals may make something different out of the same character. Bradley found Iago so intriguing in his complexity that in his account he usurps the centre of the play from Othello. F. R. Leavis, on the other hand, holds that 'we have no difficulty in taking him as we are meant to take him; and we don't (at any rate in the reading, and otherwise it's the actor's problem) ask how it is that appearance and reality can have been so successfully divorced.' Without taking up the argument about Iago, one might observe in passing that it is not improbable that if there are discontinuities in a character likely to present difficulties to an actor they will present difficulties to a reader, and that if Dr Leavis is right about Iago the part should present no unusual difficulty in performance. (For what my opinion is worth, I don't think it does.)

Of course actors vary enormously in their interpretation of great roles, partly because they differ in their understanding of the character, and partly because even the finest actor is limited in the range of possibilities he can represent. No single actor can bring out everything that Shakespeare put into Lear, Hamlet or Falstaff, just as no single pianist can bring out everything Beethoven put into his sonatas. There is no such thing as a definitive performance of a great work, but this does not mean that there are no standards by which we can judge a performance. A cringing Othello, a blustering and wholly extroverted Hamlet, a saturnine Falstaff, might conceivably bring out a single trait of character, but at the cost of falsifying the whole. What would be falsified would be, not the character alone, but the whole action, which would become incomprehensible.

The way in which the creation of a character involves irony can be clearly illustrated. There is an obvious example in Ibsen's *The Wild Duck*, where, in Act I, we see Hjalmar Ekdal at a party, very much out of his depth and ill at ease socially.

> *The Fat Guest:* Don't you think, Mr Werle, that Tokay may be considered a comparatively wholesome drink?
> *Werle:* I can guarantee the Tokay you had today, at any rate; it is one of the very finest years. And you realized that yourself, I'm sure.
> *The Fat Guest:* Yes, it had a most remarkable bouquet.
> *Hjalmar:* Is there any difference in the years?
> *The Fat Guest:* By jove, that's good!
> *Werle:* It certainly isn't worth while offering *you* a noble wine.
> *The Thin-haired Guest:* It's the same with Tokays as with photographs, Mr Ekdal. Sunshine is essential. That's true, isn't it?
> *Hjalmar:* Oh yes; the light certainly plays its part.
> *Mrs Sörby:* Why, then, it's just the same with you people at Court. You like a place in the sun too, so I've heard.

Later, in Act II, Hjalmar tells his family about the conversation, and his part in it.

> *Hjalmar:* . . . . Later on we had a little dispute about Tokay.
> *Ekdal:* Tokay, did you? That's a grand wine, that is.
> *Hjalmar:* It *can* be. But then, you know, the vintages are not all equally fine; it depends on how much sunshine the grapes have had.
> *Gina:* Why, Hjalmar, you know absolutely everything.
> *Ekdal:* And was that what they wanted to argue about?

Hjalmar: They tried to. But they were informed that it was just the same with Court officials. All vintages were not equally good in their case either – so they were told.

Gina: Well! The things you do think of!

Ekdal: Ha! Ha! So they had to put that in their pipes and smoke it!

Hjalmar: They had it, straight to their faces.

The ironic juxtaposition is comic, but not merely comic. The purpose is only partially to show up Hjalmar, for his version of the conversation, produced for a family already pre-disposed to see him in a dominant, brilliant role, is one which he already half-believes. His distortion is not the deliberate act of a hypocrite, but a necessity of his existence, of his self-respect, and the entire family are his accessories. We are missing Ibsen's point here if we fail to recognize, and feel the pathos of, a common human tendency. It is compassionate comedy, an example of the balance between sympathy and detachment which dramatic irony creates. There is less sympathy, no doubt, in Molière's portrayal of Orgon, as he tells of the religious lessons he has learnt from Tartuffe (Act I, Scene v)

> Oui, je deviens tout autre avec son entretien;
> Il m'enseigne à n'avoir affection pour rien;
> De toutes amitiés il détache mon âme;
> Et je verrais mourir frère, enfants, mère, et femme,
> Que je m'en soucierais autant que cela.

(Yes, I am entirely changed by his guidance. He teaches me to have affection for nothing, and detaches my soul from all friendships. Even if my brother, children, mother and wife were to die, I would not be in the least concerned.)

Here, of course, the irony arises from the infatuated zeal with which the lines are spoken (it is a parody of 'dying to the world') and the utter inhumanity of their implications; we do not *know* more than the speaker does, but we understand what he is saying more clearly than he does himself. We are not utterly detached, because there is a certain pathos in Orgon's naïve pride in the lesson he has learnt. For Jonson's Volpone addressing his gold we are likely to have no sympathy in this sense.

> Good morning to the day; and next, my gold!
> Open the shrine, that I may see my saint.
> Hail the world's soul, and mine! more glad than is
> The teeming earth to see the longed-for sun
> Peep through the horns of the celestial Ram,
> Am I, to view thy splendour darkening his;
> That lying here, amongst my other hoards,
> Shew'st like a flame by night, or like the day
> Struck out of chaos, when all darkness fled
> Unto the centre. O thou son of Sol,
> But brighter than thy father, let me kiss
> With adoration, thee, and every relic
> Of sacred treasure in this blessed room.
> Well did wise poets, by thy glorious name,
> Title that age which they would have the best;
> Thou being the best of things, and far transcending
> All style of joy, in children, parents, friends,
> Or any other waking dream on earth:
> Thy looks when they to Venus did ascribe,
> They should have given her twenty thousand Cupids;
> Such are thy beauties and our loves!
>
> (Act I, Scene i)

What we are seized by here is the eloquence and the passion, the intensity and richness of it – that is, our response is positive, Volpone takes us with him. Yet at the same time the language is working in another way, against Volpone, creating a critical resistance to the rich spell of his imagination. The exaltation of gold is at the expense of everything truly creative (the sun, God the creator and saviour of the Israelites, piety, natural affection and sexual love) and the speech is, in fact, a sustained blasphemy against life. Hence we are simultaneously attracted to and repelled by Volpone's vision, an equivocal attitude which can be maintained throughout the play because it is set in a world as monstrous as Volpone's imagination, but much less splendid. In this opening speech Volpone tells us more than he knows because he is insensitive to the judgement on himself which his language implies.

The preceding examples have all been major characters. Philo in *Antony and Cleopatra* is hardly a character at all, as he is not involved in the action. Yet in delivering the first thirteen lines of the play he establishes the initial situation in such a way as to foreshadow the ironic tensions which emerge in the action. He speaks three more lines at the end of the scene, and then disappears from the play, but to declare simply that he is not a character but a sort of chorus or prologue would be misleading – the kind of man he is determines what he sees and what he says.

> Nay, but this dotage of our general's
> O'erflows the measure. Those his goodly eyes,
> That o'er the files and musters of the war
> Have glowed like plated Mars, now bend, now turn,
> The office and devotion of their view
> Upon a tawny front. His captain's heart,
> Which in the scuffles of great fights hath burst
> The buckles on his breast, reneges all temper,
> And is become the bellows and the fan
> To cool a gypsy's lust. Look where they come!
> Take but good note, and you shall see in him
> The triple pillar of the world transformed
> Into a strumpet's fool. Behold and see.

In these lines we hear an authentic voice which is to be crucial in the action – the voice of Rome. We hear it again and again, primarily from Caesar, but at times even from Antony when he looks at himself through Roman eyes:

> I must from this enchanting queen break off
> Or lose myself in dotage.

It is a voice which implies a certainty and confidence of moral judgement, metallically sharp in its dismissal of weakness ('dotage', 'lust', 'strumpet') and tending towards unimaginative self-righteousness. At the same time it expresses admiration for Antony's warrior-virtues, which make him a glamorous figure even in Roman eyes. Philo is contemplating a metamorphosis which saddens him, and though there is a touch of the admonitory lecture about the way in which he calls our attention to the tableau before us, there is also a deeper feeling which emerges in 'Behold and see': we might even catch ourselves remembering the well-known passage from Lamentations – 'Behold and see if there be any sorrows like unto my sorrows.' (It is instructive to compare the Roman voice in Philo's mouth with similar speeches from Caesar's, which have a more public, less sincere ring about them.)

This, then, is what Philo is saying in expressing the sort of man he is – this is as far as a simple concern with character would take us. But if we are aware of the full ironic life of the language the speech expresses much more; implicit in it are the rival positive values of the Egyptian ethos to which Antony seems to be subdued. The opening image 'o'erflows the measure' is ambiguous: though in the context of Roman values it implies wasteful extravagance, laxity and lack of self-control, it carries other, very different implications of fruitfulness (as in the *cornucopia*) and creative generosity. Throughout the play the spirit of the Egyptian world, personified in Cleopatra, is connected with the fertility of Egypt, brought by the 'o'erflowing Nile'. The full force of these suggestions of generous richness is perhaps best conveyed in Blake's aphorism: 'The cistern contains: the fountain overflows.'

The imagery of the later lines has also an implicit significance which we can fully grasp only in the light of the action. The warrior virtues are expressed in terms of metal ('plated', 'buckles', and 'temper' which carries also the suggestion of temperance) yet significantly even in battle Antony's heart burst the restraining buckles, and the unmetallic flexibility of 'bend' and 'turn', together with the sexual overtones of 'the bellows and the fan' (compare the description by Enobarbus of Cleopatra's barge in Act II, Scene ii) convey a powerful impression of a man whose vitality may express itself in warrior virtues, but cannot be confined within them. The whole passage creates the situation, with its tension between the two worlds of the play, polarized in the persons of Caesar and Cleopatra, and warring within Antony. It brings home to us, on re-examination, the full sense in which Antony's 'legs bestrid the ocean', and the tragedy of a man who tried to express within a unified self qualities which, in the world he lived in, had declined into inexorable opposition.

III

It is possible, therefore, to make a rough but useful distinction between dramatic language expressive of character, and that which in one way or another transcends character, and determines the way in which we respond to the whole action. The concept of character is a necessary one, and to an actor the very idea of questioning its necessity would seem absurd. How, it might be asked, can one play a part without some conscious idea of the part one is playing? The question raised by Morgann in the eighteenth century, 'Was Falstaff a coward?' is certainly not irrelevant to an actor who has to play the part, since for him it takes the pressing form – 'What movement, gesture and expression are appropriate to the end of the Gadshill incident in *Henry IV*, Part I, Act II, Scene ii?' There is no escaping questions like this. But let us imagine that an actor has decided how to carry off this particular incident. We, as audience, *may* be left in no doubt how he has decided the question, but this is far from certain. We might say to the actor something like: 'You say that you had decided that Falstaff *is* a coward, yet the way you played the part did not show this.' We might, of course, be accusing him of being a bad actor, but not necessarily, because his performance might have struck us as particularly fine and 'right'. We might be saying that his idea of cowardly behaviour did not coincide with ours.

In discussing character we often too easily fall into the error of thinking that words like 'coward', 'hero', 'villain' and the host of other evaluative words we might use have a fixed and definite meaning which can be pointed to. In fact all we have in this particular case is a dramatic situation created by Shakespeare in words. Given that we can agree about the nature of that situation, our argument is really about what we mean by cowardice, though in practice we are likely to find it impossible to separate the two: disagreement about the situation and about the meaning of the concepts we are using are inseparable. All discussions of character are discussions of value, and the words we use to express value.

Literature is concerned with concepts in an entirely different way from philosophy. In literature the concern with concepts is primarily ironic, for irony is the mode of showing how the complexity of experience makes necessary a continual re-examination of our conceptual language, to check it, as it were, against the way things are, or may be. Here is a simple example of irony used in this way.

Theobald had known Dr Skinner slightly at Cambridge. He had been a burning and a shining light in every position he had filled from his boyhood upwards. He was a very great genius. Everyone knew this; they said, indeed, that he was one of the few people to whom the word genius could be applied without exaggeration. Had he not taken I don't know how many University Scholarships in his freshman's year? Had he not been afterwards Senior Wrangler, First Chancellor's Medallist, and I do not know how many more things besides? And then, he was such a wonderful speaker; at the Union debating Club he had been without a rival, and had, of course, been president; his moral character – a point on which so many geniuses were weak – was absolutely irreproachable; foremost of all, however, among his many great qualities, and perhaps more remarkable even than his genius, was what biographers have called 'the simple-minded and child-like earnestness of his character', an earnestness which might be perceived by the solemnity with which he spoke even about trifles. It is hardly necessary to say he was on the Liberal side in politics.

(Samuel Butler, *The Way of All Flesh*, Chap. XXVII)

The irony here calls attention to the way in which words like 'genius' and 'great' can be so loosely used as to be devalued, to become nothing more than a conventional seal on worldly success. It does so, however, with a repetitive insistence and a cool superiority of tone ('sneering' is the word that comes to mind) which deny to the object of irony any independent existence. Dr Skinner is reduced to a stock, representative figure, a straw man, a fraud in fact, as his career is drained of any significance it might possibly have had. This reductive irony is at the furthest possible remove from the dramatic, expressive of an egotism essentially quite as complacent as the attitude it is criticising. Whereas *this* irony impoverishes, dramatic irony enriches.

Between this kind of irony and the Shakespearian (the essence of which is perhaps expressed in Coleridge's 'myriad-minded') there are an infinite number of gradations. Consider, for instance, this poem from Blake's *Songs of Experience*.

'Love seeketh not Itself to please,
'Nor for itself hath any care,
'But for another gives its ease,
'And builds a Heaven in Hell's despair.'

So sung a little Clod of Clay
Trodden with the cattle's feet,
But a pebble of the brook
Warbled out these metres meet:

'Love seeketh only Self to please,
'To bind another to Its delight,
'Joys in another's loss of ease,
'And builds a hell in Heaven's despite.'

There is no irony of tone here; the poet's voice is utterly imperson-alized. Irony arises out of the juxtaposition, so that, by holding the two outer stanzas in balance, we are brought to realize that 'love' is not so simple as either of the songs would lead us to believe. The poem begins in the clarity of two mutually contradictory formulae, and ends in the paradoxical complexity of human experience. It is not dramatic – there is no situation, no action – but the seeds of drama are implicit in the second stanza. What is needed to turn it into drama is the transformation of the two voices into characters who would act out the meaning of their songs, confront and challenge each other in a situation out of which an action would grow.

Drama is the final extension of irony in the creative exploration of concepts. (It should go without saying that this is true only of the small proportion of drama which can be taken seriously as art.) Critics may write of 'the play of ideas', but there is no play worthy of serious consideration which is *not* a play of ideas. Certainly there are some plays which contain a great deal of discussion and argument – much of Shaw is an obvious example – but such plays will remain undramatic unless the ideas which are discussed grow out of and illuminate the life of the action, that is, unless they are embodied in characters. A play is not a debate or a discussion, any more than it is a 'pattern of imagery'. Character is not the end, but the necessary condition of drama.

IV

A dramatic character is a complex idea. The notion does not appear strange if one considers that this is also true of historical characters like Napoleon, Queen Victoria, Stalin or Hitler. How do they, in our consciousness, differ from Othello, Phèdre, John Gabriel Borkman or Macbeth? Essentially in this, that to understand the dramatic character involves understanding one complete and self-contained action which can never be changed by the discovery of new evidence; in drama, to return to Suzanne Langer's point, everything is significant within the play, and nothing is significant which is not within the play. To give a simple example, nothing we can learn about the historical Cleopatra can modify our understanding of Shakespeare's Cleopatra.

Cleopatra as an idea: 'A quibble was to him the fatal *Cleopatra* for which he lost the world, and was content to lose it' (Johnson on Shakespeare). This expresses an impoverished idea of Cleopatra, such as we find in Dryden's *All for Love, or, The World Well Lost,* but then Johnson considered that some of 'the feminine arts' of Shakespeare's Cleopatra were 'too low'. It is sad to see Johnson's lively response to Shakespeare dulled by misplaced notions of decorum.

> I saw her once
> Hop forty paces through the public street.

Enobarbus's idea of Cleopatra is part of our idea of her, and for him she is a wonder of variety, an enormous joke and a damned nuisance. To understand his famous description of her in Act II, Scene ii we have to take in the whole situation, his audience, Maecenas and Agrippa, half censorious and half fascinated, like the respectable readers of the Sunday papers, Enobarbus's man-of-the-world response to his audience ('I'll give them something to make their eyes pop!') his love of a bravura performance, and, shining through it all, an admiration which stops well this side idolatry. Enobarbus, Antony, Caesar, Charmian and Iras, the Clown, Cleopatra herself, all have their idea of Cleopatra, and out of all these grows, through our collaborative response, our idea of her, which we call Shakespeare's.

The identity of character and idea in drama needs to be demonstrated in some detail, and a relatively simple example presents itself in the role of the concept of 'honour' in *Henry IV*, Part I.

We can begin by juxtaposing three speeches delivered by Hotspur, Falstaff and Prince Hal.

Hotspur. (Act I, Scene iii)

> By heaven, methinks it were an easy leap
> To pluck bright honour from the pale-faced moon;
> Or dive into the bottom of the deep,
> Where fathom-line could never touch the ground,
> And pluck up drownèd honour by the locks;
> So he that doth redeem her thence might wear
> Without corrival all her dignities.

Falstaff. (Act V, Scene i)

Well, 'tis no matter; honour pricks me on. Yea, but how if honour prick me off when I come on? How then? Can honour set to a leg? No. Or an arm? No. Or take away the grief of a wound? No. Honour hath no skill in surgery, then? No. What is honour? A word. What is that word? Honour. What is that honour? Air. A trim reckoning! Who hath it? He that died o' Wednesday. Doth he feel it? No. Doth he hear it? No. 'Tis insensible, then? Yea, to the dead. But will it not live with the living? No. Why? Detraction will not suffer it. Therefore I'll none of it. Honour is a mere scutcheon. And so ends my catechism.

Prince Hal. (Act III, Scene ii)

> For every honour sitting on his helm,
> Would they were multitudes, and on my head
> My shames redoubled! For the time will come
> That I shall make this northern youth exchange
> His glorious deeds for my indignities.
> Percy is but my factor, good my lord,
> To engross up glorious deeds on my behalf;
> And I will call him to so strict account
> That he shall render every glory up,
> Yea, even the slightest worship of his time,
> Or I will tear the reckoning from his heart.

These speeches are not contributions to a debate, for at no point in the play do the three characters, or any two of them, *discuss* honour. Each speech is a response to a particular dramatic situation. Yet they nevertheless represent three different ways of understanding what 'honour' is, what place it has in life. That understanding is inseparable from the kind of man each speaker is, how he speaks and acts in other parts of the play, and the situation he is in when he speaks these particular words. Hotspur's speech is an intemperate outburst, an embarrassment to his companions, and an early indication of how unfitted he is for the co-operative enterprise of rebellion. He is easily carried away by his feelings, and motivated by an immature egotism which makes the quest for honour entirely competitive. The immaturity emerges in the adolescent sexuality of his fantasy of rescuing from drowning an unmistakably female personification of honour. Yet one may see all this in the passage and miss what emerges elsewhere in the play – the boyish charm, the innocent honesty and (within limits) purity of motive, the real courage. Simply to dismiss Hotspur's conception of honour is to discount these qualities.

Our initial response to Falstaff's soliloquy is likely to be one of relief; it offers a relaxing and simple dismissal of the passions, tensions and responsibilities which arise from the political action of the play, and we are likely to feel grateful for a touch of common sense and common humanity. At the same time we can hardly ignore the narrow limits which such a view of life puts on human possibilities, and which are inseparable from Falstaff's own brand of egotism. Are our sole needs limited to physical safety and comfort? Falstaff has a firm grasp of some things, but is not the life of calculated irresponsibility which he exhibits in the play, despite its exuberance of perpetual holiday, essentially ignoble *because* he can envisage no use for the conception of honour? If Falstaff is right the preoccupations of the rest of the characters are reduced to nonsense: but if this were so the whole play would be reduced to farce

Our first reaction to Hal's speech might well be critical. He is offering a rather tortuous self-exculpation to an angry and disappointed father, in which honour is considered very much as a commodity. (Note the commercial terminology – 'exchange', 'factor', 'engross', 'strict account', 'render up', 'reckoning'; Hal is saying, in modern terms, that he is about to make a take-over bid for the honour Hotspur has accumulated.) This suggestion of calculation and economy of means fits in well with the Hal we encounter in the rest of the play, and he is certainly in many ways a less attractive figure than either Hotspur or Falstaff. Yet he is far less of an egotist, and there is a note of genuine dedication here, dedication to a duty which transcends the self. If honour is a commodity to be used it is to be used in a necessary cause, and Hal cannot afford the emotional self-indulgence that Hotspur habitually allows himself, or the physical self-indulgence of Falstaff.

It is possible to imagine three distinct productions of *Henry IV*, Part I, each dedicated to the proposition that one of these three characters is 'right' about honour. It is certainly customary for academic commentators to come down on the side of Hal. '[Falstaff] views honor with a realism that contrasts with the exaggerated unreality of Hotspur's speeches on the subject and so enables Shakespeare to present the happy temperance of Prince Hal's conception' (Lily B. Campbell, *Shakespeare's Histories*, p. 244). One is moved to protest that 'realism' is not a very helpful word here; if Falstaff is a realist, is Hal less of a realist, and if so, why is it praiseworthy in him to be less than realistic? What is unreal about Hotspur's speeches? and why is Hal's temperance (a term which would have startled his father) particularly happy? Of course, no account of a successful work of literature can be as precise as the original, but there is a peculiar danger in dealing with dramatic works of disturbing a delicate balance, the subtle interrelatedness of its parts.

If you try to nail anything down, in the novel, either it kills the novel, or the novel gets up and walks away with the nail. Morality in the novel is the trembling instability of the balance. When the novelist puts his thumb in the scale, to pull down the balance to his own pre-dilection, that is immorality.

(D. H. Lawrence, *Morality and the Novel*, in *Phoenix*, p. 528)

What Lawrence, in defending implicitly the dramatic nature of the novel, here stigmatizes as immorality is the besetting sin of critics of the drama – to destroy 'the trembling instability of the balance', to simplify a subtle complexity of response. If we say that it is obvious that a successful politician should behave like Prince Hal, rather than Hotspur or Falstaff, we are pointing to the possible ways of living, feeling and thinking which a successful politician must deny himself. This involves, in human terms, gains and losses: to what extent, we might ask ourselves, does Hal's concep-tion of duty put limits on the fullness of his humanity? In entering imaginatively into the whole action of the play we are allowing questions like this to act themselves out at a level more profound than debate or discussion.

It may be useful at this point to consider what a contemporary English dramatist has had to say about the kind of distortion of which critics are capable. In an introductory note to his very interesting play *Live Like Pigs (Three Plays*, Penguin, Harmonds-worth, 1967, p. 101) John Arden writes:

When I wrote this play I intended it to be not so much a social docu-ment as a study of differing ways of life brought sharply into contact and both losing their own particular virtues under the stress of intolerance and misunderstanding. In other words, I was more con-cerned with the 'poetic' than with the 'journalistic' structure of the play. The reception of the production at the Royal Court seemed to indicate that I had miscalculated. On the one hand, I was accused by the Left of attacking the Welfare State: on the other, the play was *hailed* as a defence of anarchy and amorality. So perhaps I had better declare myself. I approve outright neither of the Sawneys nor of the Jacksons. Both groups uphold standards of conduct that are incompatible, but which are both valid in their correct context.

This brings out very well the way in which a dramatist's imagination is seized by a situation, not an argument. Any argument that arises from the play must be abstracted from it, and the process of abstraction is fraught with the possibilities of misunderstanding. Mr Arden's play is not lacking in ideas, but he is concerned to show how ideas and attitudes are *lived*. Character is the *life* of drama; as Pirandello expressed it:

> . . . every action (and every idea it contains) needs a free human personality if it is to appear live and breathing before us. It needs something that will function as its motor pathos, to use Hegel's phrase – characters, in other words.
>
> (Luigi Pirandello: *Spoken Action*, in *The Theory of the Modern Stage*, ed. Eric Bentley, Harmondsworth, 1968)

6

'Presentment': Modern Criticism and the Dramatic

If we consider the drama as a serious literary form in Western Europe we are immediately struck with the infrequency, and the brevity, of those historic periods in the life of any nation or community when great drama appears to have been possible. The span of great English drama, in the age of Shakespeare, was less than a lifetime, as was that of the French classical theatre. Greek tragedy rose and declined within a similar period. With remarkably few individual exceptions the drama of most ages, as compared with serious contemporary literature, has been trivial, false and boring. And yet (this is the remarkable fact) great writers have turned again and again to the dramatic form. Johnson, Wordsworth, Coleridge, Byron, Shelley, all wrote plays, and it was one of Keats's ambitions to produce 'a few fine plays'. Tennyson, Browning, Arnold, Hopkins and Hardy were all attracted by the form, as were Yeats, Eliot, Joyce and Lawrence. The results of all this dramatic activity are hardly striking, in contrast with the poems and novels, and there are no doubt complex artistic and social reasons why this should be so. But it remains strikingly true that the possibilities of the form continued to exert their spell at times when the omens could not have been less propitious. The present century has seen a revival of interest in serious drama which is of considerable significance, however much argument there may be as to the quality of most of the plays which have come out of it. At the same time the drama of the past has had considerable influence on non-dramatic writing and on the language of criticism. The crucial development in dramatic criticism in English was the abandonment of the procedure whereby most discussion of drama took the form of commentaries on Aristotle or (as was usually the case) commentaries on commentaries on Aristotle. From Johnson onwards the crucial question for serious criticism was not what Aristotle had said, but what Shakespeare had done, and it was not until the present century that scholars and critics were able to approach Aristotle again in a very different spirit from that of his Renaissance commentators.

The importance of Coleridge in this development is considerable, and out of all proportion to his actual achievement as a critic of Shakespeare. The spirit of Coleridge's criticism takes much of its life from the Shakespearean example, and it is no coincidence that one of his finest sustained passages of criticism (Chapter XV of *Biographia Literaria*) is an examination of Shakespeare's use of language intended to illustrate the account of imagination in the preceding chapter:

> This power . . . reveals itself in the balance or reconcilement of opposite or discordant qualities: of sameness, with difference; of the general with the concrete; the idea with the image; the individual with the representative; the sense of novelty and freshness with old and familiar objects; a more than usual state of emotion with more than usual order; judgement ever awake and steady self-possession with enthusiasm and feeling profound or vehement; . . .

Here, despite that tendency to generality which is the greatest danger of Coleridge's characteristic approach, we have what might have been the beginnings of an account of the dramatic use of language. In his actual comments on *Venus and Adonis* Coleridge comes even closer.

> It is throughout as if a superior spirit more intuitive, more intimately conscious, even than the characters themselves, not only of every

outward look and act, but of the flux and reflux of the mind in all its subtlest thoughts and feelings, were placing the whole before our view; himself meanwhile unparticipating in the passions, and actuated only by that pleasurable excitement, which had resulted from the energetic fervour of his own spirit in so vividly exhibiting what it had so accurately and profoundly contemplated. I think, I should have conjectured from these poems, that even then the great instinct, which impelled the poet to the drama, was secretly working in him. . . .

Coleridge goes on to draw attention to

... the perpetual activity of attention required on the part of the reader, from the rapid flow, the quick change, and the playful nature of the thoughts and images; and above all from the alienation, and . . . the utter *aloofness* of the poet's own feelings, from those of which he is at once the painter and the analyst; . . . . In Shakespeare's poems the creative power and the intellectual energy wrestle as in a warlike embrace. . . . At length in the drama they were reconciled. . . .

Perhaps sufficient has been quoted to establish the point that it is the dramatic qualities which he found in Shakespeare to which Coleridge the critic most deeply responded. This chapter, and occasional touches elsewhere, point towards an analysis of dramatic language which, hardly surprisingly, Coleridge never undertook; most of his successors put the stress on the individuality of Shakespeare's characters, in the manner of Hazlitt, whose vivid response to Shakespeare's plays is often a stimulating report on experience, little if at all mediated by the analytical faculty. (But see Note D, p. 90)

Matthew Arnold has been the most influential of the Victorian critics, but the little that he has to say of Shakespeare displays his weakest side. In the 'Preface' to his *Poems* of 1853, one finds the following astonishing passage – astonishing, that is, in proceeding from such a distinguished mind:

I have said that the imitators of Shakespeare, fixing their attention on his wonderful gift of expression, have directed their imitation to this, neglecting his other excellences. These excellences, the fundamental excellences of poetical art, Shakespeare no doubt possessed them – possessed many of them in a splendid degree; but it may perhaps be doubted whether even he himself did not sometimes give scope to his faculty of expression to the prejudice of a higher poetical duty. For we must never forget that Shakespeare is the great poet he is from his skill in discerning and firmly conceiving an excellent action, from his power of intensely feeling a situation, of intimately associating himself with a character; not from his gift of expression, which rather even leads him astray, degenerating sometimes into a fondness for curiosity of expression, into an irritability of fancy, which seems to make it impossible for him to say a thing plainly, even when the press of the action demands the very directest language, or its level character the very simplest.

The whole passage (there is more in the same strain) with its unthinking antithesis between action, character and situation on the one hand, and expression on the other, betrays a remarkable incapacity to grasp that it is precisely by means of his power of *dramatic* expression that Shakespeare creates the action, situation and character which Arnold claims to admire. There could be no more striking blankness in a distinguished critic – one wonders what he would have made of Hopkins!

Arnold demonstrates, at least, the extent to which the possibilities in some of Coleridge's most suggestive formulations had been missed. But in Coleridge at his best the stress fell on creative tension, 'the balance or reconcilement of opposite or discordant qualities'. Arnold's advice to the poet (the context makes it clear it is dramatic as well as narrative poetry he is thinking of) is as follows:

He will esteem himself fortunate if he can succeed in banishing from his mind all feelings of contradiction, and irritation, and impatience...

Not, be it noted, to balance or reconcile contradictions, but to *banish* them. There could be no clearer indication of how utterly undramatic was Arnold's idea of the proper language of poetry, as undramatic in its way as Johnson's.

II

A thought to Donne was an experience; it modified his sensibility. When a poet's mind is perfectly equipped for its work, it is constantly amalgamating disparate experience; the ordinary man's experience is chaotic, irregular, fragmentary. The latter falls in love, or reads Spinoza, and these two experiences have nothing to do with each other, or with the noise of the typewriter or the smell of cooking; in the mind of the poet these experiences are always forming new wholes.

(T. S. Eliot, 'The Metaphysical Poets', in Collected Essays)

I cite this passage, not to emphasize Eliot's originality (though it had when first written the force of originality) but to point to the way in which he, and other twentieth-century critics, might be said to have taken up and developed the Coleridgean hints. One might also cite the well-known passage on seventeenth-century wit: 'It involves, probably, a recognition, implicit in the expression of every experience, of other kinds of experience which are possible . . .' In his influential essays on metaphysical poetry, and the handful of early essays on the Elizabethan drama, what is being recommended is, essentially, dramatic language. Indeed, with its stress on 'impersonality', Eliot's whole theory of poetry (if he could be said to have a theory) was dramatic. Not surprisingly, his poetry, at least up to and including *The Waste Land*, has marked dramatic qualities; *Gerontion* might be cited as a particularly striking case.

Eliot was not alone, of course, in the first quarter of this century, in writing verse with a marked dramatic quality. Yeats, too, had read Donne, and the considerable change in the movement of his verse was towards the dramatic. Pound wrote dramatic monologues, and Isaac Rosenberg, that remarkably promising poet killed in the First World War, was experimenting with poetic drama. The poetry of Hopkins was finally published. What must be emphasized is that the modern critical idiom was a response to contemporary creative writing and at the same time (the two are in practice inseparable) a fresh response to qualities in the literature of the past which had been ignored, scorned, or at the least undervalued. The shift in taste, which is a weak way of putting it, went with a fresh response to Shakespeare, involving a livelier appreciation of those aspects of his art which could not be demonstrated by the nineteenth-century type of character-analysis. Eliot's criticism was a crucial factor in this shift, but the full implications of it can best be studied in the work of the critic who undoubtedly stands, in relation to our time, in an equivalent position to Johnson in his, F. R. Leavis.

III

That he has no sense of the theatre, and worse, cannot present or conceive his themes dramatically – these points are obvious. . . . Johnson – and in this he is representative of his age – has neither the gift nor the aim of capturing in words, and presenting to speak for themselves, significant particularities of sensation, perception and feeling, the significance coming out in complex total effects, which are also left to speak for themselves; he starts with general ideas and general propositions, and enforces them by discussion, comment and illustration. It is by reason of these characteristics that his verse, like that which he found most congenial, may fairly be said to have the virtues of good prose. And it seems reasonable to associate with his radically undramatic habit. . . . Johnson's concern for poetic justice, and his inability to appreciate the ways in which works of art *act* their moral judgments.

(F. R. Leavis, 'Johnson as Poet', in *The Common Pursuit*)

In quoting Dr Leavis's judgement on Dr Johnson as a *locus classicus* of modern criticism (I am sure it is that) I am not unaware of a certain irony. Few modern critics have paid less attention to drama than Dr Leavis; he has virtually nothing to say, in contrast to Wilson Knight, of drama in performance, and apart from his few essays on Shakespeare, one might search his published work in vain for any sustained examination of a play. Yet it is Dr Leavis who, more consistently than any other critic, has emphasized the dramatic nature of what, in another essay on Johnson ('Johnson and Augustanism') he calls 'the poetic-creative use of language'. He has on a number of occasions referred appreciatively to D. W. Harding's essay on Rosenberg, in particular the passage in which Professor Harding discusses Rosenberg's use of language as an extreme case of the essentially poetical use.

> Usually when we speak of finding words to express a thought we seem to mean that we have the thought rather close to formulation and use it to measure the adequacy of any possible phrasing that occurs to us, treating words as servants to the idea. 'Clothing a thought in language,' whatever it means psychologically, seems a fair metaphorical description of most speaking and writing. Of Rosenberg's work it would be misleading. He – like many poets in some degree, one supposes – brought language to bear on the incipient thought at an earlier stage of its development. Instead of the emerging idea being racked slightly so as to fit a more familiar approximation of itself, and words found for *that*, Rosenberg let it manipulate words almost from the beginning. . . . Rosenberg rarely or never illustrated his ideas by writing; he reached them through writing.
>
> (D. W. Harding, 'Aspects of the Poetry of Isaac Rosenberg', from *Exeprience into Words*, London 1963.)

(I ought to remark at this point that though I find Professor Harding's distinction useful and suggestive I have reservations about his way of putting it which Dr Leavis seems not to share. I quote it here as an essential document in the case.) This passage seems to me to point already in the direction of drama, since the dramatist, in beginning with a situation and expressing himself through characters, is allowing an idea gradually to define itself through the medium of language, is letting it *grow* rather than forcing a form upon it.

In illustrating Dr Leavis's critical practice I have found it convenient to quote from the two essays under the general heading of 'Judgment and Analysis: Notes in the Analysis of Poetry', which appeared first in *Scrutiny* (Vol XII, 1945) and are reprinted in *A Selection from Scrutiny* (Vol I, pp. 211–47). Here the stress is throughout on particularity and presentment, as when he points to

> Shelley's notable inability to *grasp* anything – to present any situation, any observed or imagined actuality, or any experience, as an object existing independently and in its own right.

Again and again one notices this stress on presented situation, and the poet's ability to create in language something which is more 'there' than a mere statement or expression of feeling. Hence the importance, approaching the work now from the reader's point of view, of not merely 'understanding', but wholly entering into the language.

> In reading a successful poem it is as if . . . one were living that particular action, situation, or piece of life.

The situation in the sense in which Dr Leavis uses the term here, is analogous to the dramatic situation, and the reader's participation is identical with that by which the audience enters into the life of dramatic characters. And just as the dramatic situation, as I have attempted to describe it, is composed of complex tension, so, in Dr Leavis's terms, is the created situation in a poem.

> It is from some such complexity as this, involving the telescoping or focal coincidence in the mind of contrasting or discrepant impressions or effects that metaphor in general – live metaphor – seems to derive its life: life involves friction and tension – a sense of arrest – in some degree.

And this generalization suggests a wider one. Whenever in poetry we come on such places of especially striking 'concreteness' – places where the verse has such life and body that we hardly seem to be reading arrangements of words – we may expect analysis to yield notable instances of the co-presence in complex effects of the disparate, the conflicting or the contrasting.

Could any account of the experience of literature point more surely in the direction of drama? 'Friction', 'tension', 'the conflicting or the contrasting'; are these not the very life of drama? And is not Dr Leavis implicitly granting, when he speaks of occasions when 'we hardly seem to be reading arrangements of words' the sense of independent life which we get from a vividly created dramatic character?

What Dr Leavis has had to say about 'wit' in seventeenth-century poetry has always seemed to me to have a particular bearing on dramatic experience.

> The activity of the thinking mind, the energy of intelligence, involved in the metaphysical habit means that, when the poet *has* urgent personal experience to deal with it is attended to and contemplated – which in turn means some kind of separation, or distinction, between experiencer and experience.

This separation, involving as it does the co-presence of a full realization of or entering-into the experience with a detached judgement of it, is, as I have tried to show, at the very centre of our complex response to dramatic action.

I have not attempted an exhaustive study of Dr Leavis's critical terminology; hardly done more, in fact, than drop a few hints which I hope may be suggestive. I might have instanced the work of other critics to bring out, for instance, the importance in modern criticism of such concepts as irony and impersonality, but the dramatic bearing of all these seems clear enough once the hint has been given. The argument would seem to be tending towards some sort of absolute claim for drama as being the furthest possible extension of irony and of the metaphorical or 'poetic-creative' use of language, some such formulation as that 'all literature aspires to the condition of drama', to parody Pater. Certainly some such idea does seem to be implicit in what I take to be the central tradition of English criticism in this century. It might be objected that such a view depends on certain critical predilections, which tell against writers (Spenser, Dryden, Shelley and Tennyson come to mind at once) who are lacking in the dramatic qualities, or traditional literary forms like the epic, the lyric and the elegaic. Certainly this is so, for the critical idiom at any time will express the prevailing taste, which is never something merely personal, but part of the intellectual air we breathe. Every new work of any importance, or any neglected work of the past, constitutes a challenge to our critical language, which might be posed in these terms: 'Can you account for me adequately in the current critical idiom? and if not, is that because of my inadequacies, or the inadequacy of your own language and preconceptions?' The language of criticism is a living language, evolving always under the pressure of particular judgements; it is not fanciful to say that the encounter between literature and the critic is in itself essentially dramatic.

7
Drama and the Novel

Drama and dramatic qualities are not confined to works written for the theatre, in the form of plays. But it was not until the nineteenth century that the possibility arose of a dramatic form capable of surpassing the drama of the theatre in depth and vitality. No one, I imagine, would be disposed to question that the novel has been, at least for the last hundred years, the major literary form; there might be protests at the claim that it has been the major dramatic form, though this conclusion is difficult to avoid. The novel was the irregular offspring of the essay and the drama, and the nineteenth-century novel in particular owes more to Shakespeare and the Greek tragedians than has ever been fully acknowledged. George Eliot was never again so explicit in her indebtedness to Aeschylus as she is in *Adam Bede*, but the influence remained a powerful one; her debt to Shakespeare is perhaps less obvious, though it might be brought out in a consideration of the relationship between *Silas Marner* and *The Winter's Tale*. Dickens had an abiding interest in the early English drama, and the link with Ben Jonson has often been remarked on. Henry James, the novelist *par excellence*, was a fascinated and intelligent student of drama (his theatre criticism repays study) and in attempting to exclude as far as possible the narrative intrusions of the author's own distinctive voice, most particularly in *The Awkward Age*, he set an example which other novelists have tried to follow. The novel can, however, never be *purely* dramatic; it must be descriptive, narrative, discursive, too, for as Lawrence remarked, 'You can put anything you like in a novel.' Yet if the novel is never purely dramatic, it is essentially so. It is not a quibble to say that the novel is not a narrative form with dramatic moments, but a dramatic form within a narrative framework.

The action of a novel takes place on a shifting stage. The narrative passages are the means by which the stage is shifted, the descriptive passages the means by which the stage is set. The novelist has two resources not available to the dramatist proper: the reflective comment in his own voice, and the interior consciousness of one or more of his characters. In addition he has to do some of the work of the actor (gesture, movement, facial expression, etc.) much of which the modern playwright indicates by stage directions. In the case of interior consciousness the novelist is, of course, merely extending the resources of the soliloquy.

> Gwendolen sank on the settee, clasped her hands, and looked straight before her, not at her mother. She had the expression of one who had been startled by a sound and was listening to know what would come of it. The sudden change of the situation was bewildering. A few minutes before she was looking along an inescapable path of repulsive monotony, with hopeless inward rebellion against the imperious lot which left her no choice: and lo, now, a moment of choice was come. Yet – was it triumph she felt most or terror? Impossible for Gwendolen not to feel some triumph in a tribute to her power at a time when she was first tasting the bitterness of insignificance: again she seemed to be getting a sort of empire over her own life. But how to use it? Here came the terror. Quick, quick, like pictures in a book beaten open with a sense of hurry, came back vividly, yet in fragments, all that she had gone through in relation to Grandcourt – the allurements, the vacillations, the resolve to accede, the final repulsion; the incisive face of that dark-eyed lady with the lovely boy; her own pledge (was it a pledge not to marry him?) – the new disbelief in the worth of men and things for which that scene of disclosure had become a symbol. That unalterable experience made a vision at which in the first agitated moment, before tempering reflections could suggest themselves, her native terror shrank.
>
> Where was the good of choice coming again? What did she wish?

Anything different? No! and yet in the dark seed-growths of consciousness a new wish was forming itself – 'I wish I had never known
it!' Something, anything she wished for that would have saved her
from the dread to let Grandcourt come.

(George Eliot, Daniel Deronda, Chapter 26, Penguin edn,
Harmondsworth, 1967, p. 336)

The sense of agitation vividly conveyed, the frantic hope for a
loop-hole to escape from conscience, the desire for 'empire', the
bitter disillusionment, all these and so much more are conveyed
here with a dramatic life of presentment and tension such as might
well remind us of, say, Macbeth's 'If it were done when 'tis
done . . .' The passage exhibits the kind of dramatic power we find
in the great dramatists, and which we quite clearly do *not* find in
(say) Defoe or Fielding. To call this narrative would plainly be
absurd, and to deny it the status of great dramatic writing would
be merely to be befuddled by archaic categories. We enter into
this experience, we are not told about it.

The differences between the novelist and the playwright are
obvious enough. If the dramatist is required to hold his audience's
attention and engagement more continuously than the novelist, he
has to do it for a shorter time, and with the assistance of the actual
physical presence of his action. And so on and so on. In asserting
the common essence of the novelist's and dramatist's art I do not
ignore the many ways in which the necessary differences in the
conditions of their art separate them. But one of the important
tasks of criticism is to remove or modify distinctions which stand
in the way of an apprehension of the most significant connections –
the important question to ask is, if Shakespeare had been born in
(say) 1820, would he have been a novelist or a playwright? There
seems to me to be only one answer.

It would be impossible here to illustrate the full dramatic range
of which the novel is capable, and it is hardly necessary. *Mutatis
mutandis*, almost everything of significance that can be said about

plays can be said about novels. It is probably in *pace* that they differ most; the novelist can develop his action in a more leisurely manner. The greater part of Chapter X in Jane Austen's *Mansfield Park*, for instance, is dialogue with only the minimum of authorial guidance. It presents one of the book's crucial scenes, defining by inference Mr Crawford's relation to the Bertram sisters (the whole business with the key has very significant implications, which are allowed to emerge in an entirely dramatic manner, with no prompting from the novelist) and the effect on Fanny, as well as on Edmund himself, of Edmund's being increasingly attracted to Mary Crawford. The ironies of the passage have nothing to do with *tone*. The dialogue (almost uninterrupted for four pages of my edition) is thoroughly natural and 'right' – one would not have it otherwise. Yet one doubts whether it would be sufficient to hold the attention of a theatre audience. It lacks pace, concentration, and local vividness. Similarly, although James's *The Awkward Age* is largely composed of dialogue, one cannot imagine its being successfully acted. (It is interesting to note that a television adaptation of James's *Portrait of a Lady*, which remained very faithful to James's dialogue, was a considerable success, whereas James himself failed lamentably as a playwright.)

The dramatic function of dialogue, then, varies somewhat in the novel and the drama. But of course the drama of the novel is not so dependent on dialogue, and it is possible for the novelist to create an extremely dramatic scene without dialogue. In Chapter IV of D. H. Lawrence's *The Rainbow* (p. 122 in the Penguin edition) there is a scene, complex and powerful in its effect, between Anna and Will Brangwen, stooking sheaves in the moonlight.

> They worked together, coming and going, in a rhythm, which carried their feet and their bodies in tune. She stooped, she lifted the burden of sheaves, she turned her face to the dimness where he was, and went with her burden over the stubble. She hesitated, set down her sheaves,

there was a swish and hiss of mingling oats, he was drawing near, and she must turn again. And there was the flaring moon laying bare her bosom again, making her drift and ebb like a wave.

He worked steadily, engrossed, threading backwards and forwards like a shuttle across the strip of cleared stubble, weaving the long line of riding shocks, nearer and nearer to the shadowy trees, threading his sheaves with hers.

And always, she was gone before he came. As he came, she drew away, as he drew away, she came. Were they never to meet?

The effect of the whole passage is of an increasing dramatic tension, as Will strives, by increasing his pace, to bring them together. It is a ritual drama completely without words, in a context every detail of which is significant, and its effect reminds me of accounts of primitive dramatic rituals; a sense of the power and mystery of life for which no abstract formulation would be an adequate substitute. It must be emphasized that this is not descriptive or narrative writing; although belonging in a sense to Suzanne Langer's 'virtual past' it has all the immediacy of a present happening, as if it were being acted out before us. Possibly the nearest one could come to it on the modern stage is the ballet.

II

The novel has not 'superseded' the drama, except in the sense that it has replaced it as the most popular literary form. It evolved from the drama, no doubt, chiefly as a result of social changes which began with the gradual social stratification of audiences in the early seventeenth century, and the gradual emergence of the possibilities of modern privacy in the eighteenth. It is a form more flexible and various than anything possible in the theatre, in which most of the greatest writers of the past century have chosen to express themselves.

But the fact that the theatre has not only survived but to some extent revived is also a fact for which there are social explanations. Drama is essentially collaborative: it is a collaboration between the dramatist on the one hand and the players on the other; between the players themselves; and between the players and the audience. (See Note E, p. 92.) It is an activity in a far broader sense than reading a novel can be, and it creates, albeit briefly, a sense of communal experience which is perhaps the nearest most people today can come to a shared ritual. It keeps us in vital contact with the great drama of the past, and at least holds open the possibility of a great drama in the future. But drama is of all the arts the most vulnerable, the least hardy, subject to all kinds of vulgarizing pressure, most directly subject to economic necessity and most easily depressed by corrupt and fashionable tastes. Most major dramatists have been, as Ibsen was, increasingly alienated from the theatre which remained their only medium. The attempt to make the theatre once again a medium for the finest and most profound literary expression will no doubt continue to be undertaken, but the odds will remain fearsomely against success. One can only admire those who persist in the attempt, scorning the cheaper (if more profitable) satisfactions the theatre can provide.

Note A: Decorum

It is probably too late to reinstate 'decorum' as a live critical term, which is unfortunate. It has become too closely associated with the neoclassical categorizing criticism, with its insistence that every work of literature belonged to a particular 'kind', and must be bound by the general rules applying to that 'kind'. It belongs, too, to an age in which the social sense of 'decorum' was still a living force. The history of the theatre in France is rich with occasions on which an audience has expressed its disapproval of what it held to be breaches of decorum, like the celebrated first night of Hugo's *Hernani*. However, the romantic notion of decorum as a mere clog on inspiration is quite misleading, and probably has its origins in the eighteenth-century idea of Shakespeare as an inspired natural genius ('native wood-notes wild') somehow miraculously exempted from the 'rules of art'.

Every play, in a sense, establishes its own decorum, partly by demonstrating in itself the conventions within which it is to be judged, partly by placing itself in a particular relation to other plays. (So that we might say after a quarter of an hour in the theatre, 'Ah, this is a farce.') Certain dramatic effects can be achieved by breaches of decorum, or by leaving the audience uncertain as to what kind of play it is they are witnessing – like 'playing in the cracks'. But these effects depend on a sense of decorum; a theatre of the absurd could not exist without a theatre which was not absurd, and 'black comedy' would be a meaningless term if we did not have a general notion of what comedy was. In a world which was as absurd as some theorists of absurdity say it is, absurd theatre would be impossible.

Note B: Destiny

The passage quoted (see p. 29) continues: 'That is Destiny.'

It is impossible in discussing drama to avoid concepts like 'Fate' and 'Destiny', since, particularly when tragedy is under consideration, they can foster all sorts of misunderstanding. For instance, Suzanne Langer continues: 'Destiny is, of course, always a virtual phenomenon – there is no such thing in cold fact.' Here 'thing' and 'cold fact' quite fog the issue, as I think does 'phenomenon'. Destiny is a mode of understanding, and we can talk of it in connection with real life (which is full of facts at all temperatures). The same series of facts might lead one observer to talk of Destiny, whereas another might pooh-pooh the idea. The difference between the two would be in the sense, or lack of sense, they made of what they observed, and the first observer would be pointing to a certain fitness or rightness in the outcome of events. When Donne says to his mistress:

> If ever any beauty I did see
> Which I desired, and got, 'twas but a dream of thee

he is expressing with more precision and force the feeling lovers have that they were 'meant' for each other. He is not saying that he knew before, or should have known, that such was to be the case. In life a sense of Destiny is necessarily retrospective. But in drama, since everything is put before us to be understood, it is impossible to distinguish between what happens and the sense we make of it, since for each of us what happens *is* the sense we make of it. The sense of Destiny is not merely retrospective because we know we are witnessing a whole action, and our idea of what that whole action will be (or perhaps *is*) is gradually shaping itself. This is the meaning of 'necessity' in drama; to feel the fitness of a certain dénouement is not to believe that nothing else could possibly have happened – Lear *might* have died of exposure in the storm scene, and that possibility, too, is part of what we make of the action.

Of course, characters in plays may talk of Fate or Destiny, and this becomes part of our understanding of them and their world. This is particularly the case with the forebodings of Greek tragedy. On the other hand, when we look back from the end of *Romeo and Juliet*, we may remember Romeo's words at the end of Act I, Scene iv.

> . . . my mind misgives
> Some consequence yet hanging in the stars,
> Shall bitterly begin his fearful date
> With this night's revels, and expire the term
> Of a despised life closed in my breast,
> By some vile forfeit of untimely death.

We could say that this is perfectly in character with the melancholy Romeo who is the mooning lover of Rosaline, but to connect this with the prologue's 'a pair of star-crossed lovers', and make Romeo's speech a premonition hardly helps us to make sense of the dénouement. We might argue about the role of this speech in the play, and could conclude that it is a rather clumsy hint on Shakespeare's part, an attempt to give a rather conventionally tragic dimension to the pathos of the closing scene, which is in fact the result of coincidence and sheer carelessness. When, on the other hand, Lady Macbeth says to her husband in Act I, Scene v:

> Thy letters have transported me beyond
> This ignorant present, and I feel now
> The future in the instant,

she is certainly expressing her feeling that Macbeth is destined to be king, but this feeling is inseparable from determination. But the future which the play brings is something far more terrible than she is imagining, and it is our sense of the Destiny working out in the play which invests these lines with their awful irony. This sense of Destiny *is* the ultimate irony of great drama, and it is never fully shared by the characters.

Note C: Action, Plot and Structure

All these three terms are used in a bewildering variety of ways which it is not feasible to discuss here. 'Action' is of course ambiguous, and must include what is actually happpening at any given time in the play. But it is also the whole play, considered as that to which any given moment, situation or speech is to be related in order to be fully understood. There are considerable dangers in abstracting the 'action' as a whole from a consideration of those relationships. It is our full understanding of the whole, and cannot exist apart from that understanding; we are aware of it particularly in our sense of the 'rightness' of any particular part.

There have been many attempts to distinguish between 'action' and 'plot', some of which I do not understand. But plot seems to be used in common parlance to indicate a consecutive account of the events of the play (or of a novel) which is abstracted as far as possible from the significance of those events. (The 'plot' of a great play can be recounted pretty faithfully and yet with ludicrous effect; I remember a 'turn' in which Sir Bernard Miles did it with *Hamlet*.) I see no good reason for disturbing accepted usage, though no doubt there are Aristotelians who will disagree. Aristotle's dictum that plot is the 'soul' of drama is certainly an instance of using 'plot' where I would use 'action'.

'Structure' belongs more clearly under the general heading of technique, and refers to the identifiable means by which a dramatist relates the parts of the play to each other and to the whole, and keeps before our attention what is most central to the action.

Note D: Hazlitt and Keats

Hazlitt, in the third of his *Lectures on the English Poets,* has this to say of Shakespeare.

> The striking peculiarity of Shakespeare's mind was its generic quality, its power of communication with all other minds – so that it contained a universe of thought and feeling within itself, and had no one peculiar bias, or exclusive excellence more than another. He was just like any other man, but that he was like all other men. He was the least of an egotist that it was possible to be. He was nothing in himself; but he was all that others were, or that they could become. . . . He had only to think of anything in order to become that thing, with all the circumstances belonging to it.

Writing of Wordsworth, on the other hand, he remarks that

> All accidental varieties and individual contrasts are lost in an endless continuity of feeling, like drops of water in the ocean-stream! An intense intellectual egotism swallows up every thing. . . . But the evident scope and tendency of Mr Wordsworth's mind is the reverse of dramatic.
>
> *(Observations on Mr Wordsworth's Poem 'The Excursion')*

The distinction Hazlitt makes here is interesting and up to a point valid, though in the end it presents the same kind of difficulties as T. S. Eliot's distinction between 'the man who suffers and the mind which creates' in *Tradition and the Individual Talent,* difficulties which are considered in F. R. Leavis's essay on Eliot's criticism in *'Anna Karenina' and other Essays.* (See in particular pp. 178–81.)

Hazlitt's distinction has influenced modern criticism almost entirely through the medium of Keats's letters, and in particular the phrase 'negative capability.' Keats thus characterizes a quality 'which Shakespeare possessed so enormously' and which enables a man to be capable of 'being in uncertainties, Mysteries, doubts, without any irritable reaching after fact & reason. . . .' In a later letter he writes:

> As to the poetical Character itself, (I mean that sort of which, if I am anything, I am a Member; that sort distinguished from the words-worthian or egotistical sublime; which is a thing per se and stands alone) it is not itself – it has no self – it is everything and nothing – It has no character – it enjoys light and shade; it lives in gusto, be it foul or fair, high or low, rich or poor, mean or elevated – It has as much delight in conceiving an Iago as an Imogen. . . . A Poet is the most unpoetical of anything in existence; because he has no Identity – he is continually infor[ming?] – and filling some other Body. . . .
>
> (Letter to Richard Woodhouse 27 October 1818)

This unegotistical and, in Hazlitt's sense, dramatic quality Keats identified with his own capacity for imaginative empathy, which emerges strikingly in his poetry. It is worth remarking that *The Eve of St Agnes* is conceived and executed almost entirely in dramatic terms.

Note E: Collaboration

Drama is the most collaborative of literary forms. But a sharp distinction needs to be drawn between collaboration and participation. All art keeps a certain distance, and the fact that we are drawn into drama so intensely makes the preservation of that distance more, not less important. 'Audience participation', 'total theatre' or any similar formula implies an abolition of that distance, which is destructive of drama. Certainly the origins of drama were in ritual, which implies participation, but it was not until the play and the audience were completely separated that drama emerged. (Football originated in ritual, too, but spectators who wish to participate are quickly removed from the field of play.) Paradoxically, to enter into the world and action of a play we must remain outside it, and any invitation to 'join in' destroys the integrity of the world and the action. This remains true whatever the shape of the stage, and however the audience is arranged before it or around it. 'Total theatre' may be interesting, exciting, or even therapeutic; it may fulfil a genuine social need; but it is not drama.

Bibliography

I

ARISTOTLE'S *Poetics*, which includes the most influential of all discussions of drama, is available in many translations; that of Bywater (Oxford, 1909) is usually considered the most reliable. There is a translation and extended commentary in S. H. BUTCHER'S *Aristotle's Theory of Poetry and Fine Art* (London, 1895), an interesting attempt to understand the work in the terms of nineteenth-century criticism. A translation by T. S. DORSCH is available in the Penguin, *Classical Literary Criticism* (1965). There are useful summaries of Aristotle's influence on Renaissance dramatic theory in J. E. SPINGARN'S *A History of Literary Criticism in the Renaissance* (New York, rev. ed, 1908) and J. W. H. ATKINS'S *English Literary Criticism: the Renascence* (London, 1947).

Of considerable historical importance are DRYDEN'S *Of Dramatic Poesy* which is collected with other essays in the two-volume Everyman edition (London, 1962) and CORNEILLE'S *Writings on the Theatre* (ed. H. T. Barnwell, Oxford, 1965). There are two convenient collections of JOHNSON'S Shakespearian criticism: *Johnson on Shakespeare* (ed. W. Raleigh, Oxford, 1908) and *Dr Johnson on Shakespeare* (ed. W. K. Wimsatt, Penguin edn, Harmondsworth, 1968). COLERIDGE'S *Biographia Literaria,* of which Chapter XV is of particular interest, is in Everyman's Library (ed. G. Watson, London, 1956) as is his *Shakespearean Criticism* (2 vols, ed. T. M. Raysor, London, 1960). Also available is *Coleridge on Shakespeare* (ed. T. Hawkes, Harmondsworth, 1959).

Hazlitt's essays mentioned in Note D are in volumes 4 and 5 of his *Complete Works* (ed. Howe, London, 1930) and a full discussion of Keats's indebtedness to Hazlitt can be found in Chapter X ('Negative Capability') of W. J. BATE'S *John Keats* (Oxford, 1964). ARNOLD'S *Preface* to the 1853 edition of his *Poems* can be found in most modern editions of his poetry, and under the title 'On the Choice of Subjects in Poetry', in the World's Classics collection *English Critical Essays (Nineteenth Century)* (Oxford, 1916). The essays on drama and seventeenth-century poetry in T. S. ELIOT'S *Selected Essays* (London, 1932) are of particular importance.

The writings of F. R. LEAVIS which have a particular bearing on the subject are: Chapter I of *Revaluation* (London, 1936; Penguin edn., Harmondsworth, 1964);

'Johnson and Augustanism', 'Johnson as Poet' and 'Tragedy and the "Medium"' in *The Common Pursuit* (London, 1952);

'T. S. Eliot as Critic' and 'Johnson as Critic' in *'Anna Karenina' and other Essays* (London, 1967);

'Eliot's "Axe to Grind" and the Nature of Great Criticism' in *English Literature in Our Time and the Universities* (London, 1969);

'Judgment and Analysis: Notes in the Analysis of Poetry' in *A Selection from 'Scrutiny'* (Cambridge, 1968);

'Antony and Cleopatra' and 'All for Love', *Scrutiny* Vol. V, No. 2 (1936).

Versions of the last two items can be found in Dr. Leavis's *The Living Principle* (London, 1975).

D. W. Harding, *Experience into Words* (London, 1963).

Literary Criticism: a Short History, by W. K. WIMSATT and CLEANTH BROOKS (New York, 1957) is useful, though the 'slant' is markedly, and at times misleadingly, American.

II

H. GRANVILLE-BARKER'S *Prefaces to Shakespeare* (2 vols,

London, 1958) are the most successful sustained attempt to consider Shakespeare's plays in the light of a knowledge of the theatre of his time and the considerable theatrical experience of the author himself. G. WILSON KNIGHT, the most important Shakespearian critic of his time, is essential reading: of particular importance are *The Wheel of Fire* (rev. edn, London, 1949; University Paperback edn, London, 1960) and *Principles of Shakespearean Production* (London, 1964; enlarged edition as *Shakespearean Protion*, London, 1968). His approach to Shakespeare may profitably be compared with that of A. C. BRADLEY in *Shakespearean Tragedy* (London, 1904; Paperback edn, 1965) as may also the approach of L. C. KNIGHTS in 'How Many Children Had Lady Macbeth?' which is collected in *Explorations* (London, 1946; Penguin edn., Harmondsworth, 1964). This last essay includes a useful brief account of the development of the 'character-analysis' mode of Shakespeare criticism. Two other interesting modern considerations of the place of 'character' in the criticism of Shakespeare are A. B. SEWELL'S *Character and Society in Shakespeare* (Oxford, 1951) and J. I. M. STEWART'S *Character and Motive in Shakespeare* (London, 1949).

The first part of M. C. BRADBROOK'S *Themes and Conventions of Elizabethan Tragedy* (Cambridge, 1935) is a useful introduction to the conventions of the drama of Shakespeare's time, and MADELEINE DORAN'S *Endeavours of Art* (Madison, Wis., 1954) is an attempt to relate the theory and practice of Elizabethan and Jacobean drama which is at once scholarly and lively.

III

The most intelligent contemporary critic of drama in the theatre is ERIC BENTLEY, any of whose books can be recommended. *The Life of the Drama* (London, 1965) is certainly the most stimulating work on the theory of drama currently available. H. GRANVILLE-

BARKER'S *On Dramatic Method* (London, 1931; republished, London, 1960) is an excellent brief introduction, and there are also *The Frontiers of Drama* by UNA ELLIS-FERMOR (London, 1945; paperback edn., 1964) and *The Theatre and Dramatic Theory* by ALLARDYCE NICOLL (London, 1962). Two works in which drama is approached in a more philosophical manner are SUZANNE K. LANGER'S *Feeling and Form* (London, 1953) in which Chapter 17 is of particular interest, and R. PEACOCK'S *The Art of Drama* (London, 1957). *Perspectives on Drama*, edited by J. L. CALDERWOOD and H. E. TOLLIVER (Oxford, 1968) is a useful, if uneven, collection of writings on drama from a great variety of points of view. It includes the relevant chapter from *Feeling and Form*, and stimulating essays by HENRI GHÉON on 'The Conditions of Dramatic Art', and by FRIEDRICH DÜRRENMATT on 'Problems of the Theatre'.

W. B. YEATS was, as well as a great poet, a man much concerned with the theatre, many of his reflections upon which can be found in the collection of essays published under the title *Explorations* (London, 1962).

IV

There are a great number of books on practical theatrical matters, and the history of the theatre, most of which have little bearing on drama as literature. Eric Bentley's collection *The Theory of the Modern Stage* (Penguin edn., Harmondsworth, 1968) is a useful introduction to the variety of theories about drama which have been current and influential in the last hundred years, and N. MARSHALL'S *The Producer and the Play* (London, 1957) covers much the same ground in an intelligent and readable account of the emergence of the producer as an important figure in the life of the theatre. Allardyce Nicoll's *World Drama* (London, 1949) is extremely comprehensive, and BAMBER GASCOIGNE'S *World*

Theatre (London, 1968) can be recommended for its superb illustrations.

Not much can be learnt from reprinted theatre criticisms of productions one has not seen, but there are available useful collections of the theatre reviews of G. B. SHAW (*Our Theatres in the Nineties*, 3 vols, London, 1932) and HENRY JAMES (*The Scenic Art*, London, 1949). There is also a selection of *Shaw on Shakespeare* (ed. E. Wilson, Harmondsworth, 1969).

It should go without saying that the best way to learn about drama is to read the great dramatists, and to see their plays in performance as often as possible.

Index